GIRTON COLLEGE STUDIES

EDITED BY LILIAN KNOWLES, LITT.D., READER IN ECONOMIC HISTORY
IN THE UNIVERSITY OF LONDON

No. 6

PRAGMATISM AND
FRENCH VOLUNTARISM

THESIS APPROVED FOR THE DEGREE
OF MASTER OF ARTS
IN THE UNIVERSITY OF LONDON, 1912

PRAGMATISM AND FRENCH VOLUNTARISM

WITH ESPECIAL REFERENCE TO THE NOTION
OF TRUTH IN THE DEVELOPMENT OF
FRENCH PHILOSOPHY FROM MAINE
DE BIRAN TO PROFESSOR BERGSON

BY

L. SUSAN STEBBING, M.A.

TUTOR AND LECTURER KING'S COLLEGE FOR WOMEN
VISITING LECTURER GIRTON COLLEGE

Cambridge:
at the University Press
1914

CAMBRIDGE
UNIVERSITY PRESS

University Printing House, Cambridge CB2 8BS, United Kingdom

Published in the United States of America by Cambridge University Press, New York

Cambridge University Press is part of the University of Cambridge.

It furthers the University's mission by disseminating knowledge in the pursuit of
education, learning and research at the highest international levels of excellence.

www.cambridge.org
Information on this title: www.cambridge.org/9781107626638

© Cambridge University Press 1914

First published 1914
First paperback edition 2013

A catalogue record for this publication is available from the British Library

ISBN 978-1-107-62663-8 Paperback

PREFACE

THE keen and widespread interest of all classes of readers in the philosophy of Bergson—an interest that was increased by his visits to the Universities of Oxford, Birmingham and London—shows no sign of diminishing. The enthusiasm with which the 'New Philosophy' was at first welcomed seems, however, to be setting in the opposite direction, and the excessive praise and indiscriminating acceptance of his doctrines have now given place to a criticism no less indiscriminating and, perhaps, equally unjustifiable.

In the present state of public opinion, therefore, I venture to offer this essay which, although written from a so-called 'intellectualistic' standpoint diametrically opposed to M. Bergson's, is nevertheless not blind to the interest and importance of his work.

It is the fashion among present day philosophers to depreciate reason, and in the forefront of these are the French Voluntarists—especially the Bergsonian Intuitionists—and the Pragmatists. But in their methods and conclusions they are obviously opposed and an attempt is made to show that in no sense can the French Voluntarists be classed as Pragmatists. In their treatment of the problem of truth this divergence becomes marked. Both, however, fail to give a satisfactory account of truth, the Pragmatist because he identifies truth with one of its consequences, the Bergsonian Intuitionist because he identifies truth with reality. Hence both resort to non-intellectual methods of determining truth and of solving metaphysical problems. But only, it is urged, by the admission of the non-existential character of truth and by the complete working out of the demands of intellect can we obtain knowledge that is at once complete and rational, hence truly *knowledge.*

In the original form this essay, written during the course of 1911 and completed in the early days of 1912, was submitted to the University of London and gained for its author the degree of Master of Arts. Only a few verbal alterations have been made in the essay itself, quotations have for the most part been translated, and the bibliography has been enlarged and brought up to date. In a paper, entitled "The Notion of Truth in Bergson's Theory of Knowledge," read by the author before the Aristotelian Society in May 1913 some part of this essay was reproduced and has since appeared in the *Proceedings* of the Society.

In conclusion, I wish to thank the Rev. Professor Caldecott for his valuable help and kind encouragement during the writing of this essay and its preparation for the press, and also Miss E. E. C. Jones, Mistress of Girton College, and the Council whose grant made the publication of it possible.

L. S. S.

LONDON,
January 14th, 1914.

CONTENTS

ABBREVIATIONS USED.

R.M.M. ...	...	...	Revue de Métaphysique et de Morale.
B.S.F.Ph.	...	...	Bulletin de la Société française de philosophie.
Rv. phil. ...	...	...	Revue philosophique.
D.I.C. ...	*Bergson*		Essai sur les Données immédiates de la Conscience.
M. et M. ...	,,		Matière et Mémoire.
Ev. Cr. ...	,,		L'Evolution Créatrice.
P.C. ...	,,		La Perception du Changement.
Essais ...	*Renouvier*		Essais de Critique Général. (2nd Ed.)
Dil. de la Mét.	,,		Les Dilemmes de la métaphysique pure.
Lib. et Dét.	*Fouillée*		La Liberté et le Déterminisme.
Ps. des I.-f.	,,		Psychologie des Idées-forces.
Evol. des I.-f.	,,		Evolutionnisme des Idées-forces.

I. INTRODUCTION

THE philosophy of the present age, no less than its politics, is characterised by the prevailing spirit of democracy, hence by a hatred of authority, a passion for equality and, finally, by a tendency to bring all questions in the last resort to the arbitrament of force.

The basis of democracy is the recognition of the worth of man as man, irrespective of social status, work or capacity. A "government" is worthy of obedience and respect only if it embody the "choice of the people"; there are none so low nor ignorant that they should be denied a voice in the government of their country. The will of the majority must be made to prevail, by force if necessary. In other words, the struggle for existence must be admitted in so far as all who "survive" are to be accounted equally "fit," but is to be condemned in so far as it involves the elimination of the unfit. This contradiction which lies at the heart of democracy is curiously repeated and illustrated in pragmatic philosophy which, partially derived from the anti-democratic philosophy of Nietzsche, is yet a striking outcome of the democratic demand for a purely "human" philosophy of life—a "Humanism" based upon the actual interests and emotions of mankind.

The latter part of the nineteenth century has consequently witnessed the reaction of this ideal upon philosophy which has been gradually permeated with the democratic spirit. No longer must philosophy remain "within the closet"; it must be brought down to the "plain man" whose appeal has lately been so eloquently uttered. It is, indeed, instructive to compare the sentiment expressed by Prof. Jacks in *The Bitter Cry of the Plain Man*[1], with the intellectual aloofness of Mr Bradley's standpoint. Philosophy, says Mr Bradley, must always remain an affair of the intellect; it "will always be hard[2]." In revolt against such a view the "plain man" as represented by Prof. Jacks, appalled by the "supremely forbidding" character of the Hegelian dialectic, protests that "if the truths most important to men explain themselves in this manner, then our lot in this world is dismal in the extreme[3]," and he makes his appeal to philosophers,—"Is it beneath you gentlemen, to attend to these by-products of your work, to study the effect of your potions not only on some isolated nerve of the intellect, but as affecting the vital pulse of the human heart?"

The protest that philosophy has been made too hard for the plain man does not confine itself to condemnation of technicalities of language and the uncouthness of German philosophical terminology, but becomes a plea for the recognition of other attitudes towards the Universe than that of regarding it as a "problem-to-be-solved." Life, it is urged, is more than intellect, hence a rational explanation of the Universe could not suffice to satisfy the

---

[1] Jacks, *Alchemy of Thought.*

[2] *Mind*, N. S. 51, p. 335.

[3] *loc. cit.* p. 24.

philosopher as a man; his whole emotional reaction must be taken into account.

Over the philosophers themselves is passing a wave which leads them to bring philosophy into contact with life, to invest it with the charm of personality, and to breathe life into the "dead bones of metaphysics." The natural outlet of this wave is some form of "Voluntarism" which shall lay stress on the active, volitional side of man by denying that intellect is the sole guide to, and judge of truth, or even the dominant factor in its construction. Intellect must not only be dethroned from its proud position as sovereign in philosophy; it must henceforth assume its rightful place as a mere instrument for the furtherance of human activity.

There is a further force at work to revolutionize the philosopher's attitude. The too complete success of the mechanical sciences in the early part of the nineteenth century, coupled with the recognition of the reign of natural law in the animal kingdom brought about mainly by Darwin's *Origin of Species*, has led to a revolt against that mechanical conception of the Universe that reduces it to the dead level of matter in motion and looks for the progress of science in "the extension of the province of what we call matter and causation, and the concomitant gradual banishment from all regions of human thought of what we call spirit and spontaneity[1]."

This "nightmare" conception—to use Huxley's own expression—has provoked a reaction against science as the construction of intellect on the one hand, and on the other—most markedly in France—has led to the admission of contingency into the realm of physical science itself.

[1] Huxley, *Collected Essays*, I. p. 159.

This reaction from a rigid, all-pervading determinism to radical contingency we shall find to be characteristic of French Voluntarism; it is, indeed, in France that the "philosophy of contingency" first attained clear and complete expression.

We find, then, in contemporary philosophy two tendencies: on the one hand a tendency to bring philosophy into closer touch with life and to put contingency everywhere so as to ensure our finding freedom in man; on the other hand a tendency to disparage intellect as the faculty of conceptual knowledge and to turn to some higher form of "perception" as giving a direct contact with reality.

In Pragmatism—whether it be regarded as "epistemological utilitarianism of the worst sort," or merely as a theory of the manipulation of data for the purposes of science—these two tendencies are closely connected. Disparagement of intellect is here an outcome of the desire to bring philosophy down into the arena of "the drudgery and commonplace that are our daily portion[1]," by laying stress on the emotional rather than on the intellectual aspects of life, regarding intellect only as a means to the satisfaction of other needs of man. The end is doing, not knowing. Knowledge is subservient to action and what is useful in the way of conduct becomes the supreme criterion of its trustworthiness. In French Voluntarism, however, the condemnation of intellect is based upon the alleged inability of the intellect to resolve the Kantian antinomies and Zenonian paradoxes that result from the conception of time as a

---

[1] Schiller, *Humanism*, p. 17.

continuum, while the assertion of universal contingency appears to be the outcome of a radically anti-intellectualistic temporalism.

Pragmatism, which frequently claims to be only an epistemological method compatible with the most varied metaphysics, originated in a rule first formulated in the interests of clear thinking by the American mathematician, Mr C. S. Peirce. In his posthumous work James sums it up thus: "The pragmatic rule is that the meaning of a concept may always be found, if not in some sensible particular which it directly designates, then in some particular difference in the course of human experience which its being true will make."

According to James' earlier statements the doctrine may be summed up: the *practical* bearings of a concept constitute its whole meaning and value. This later substitution of "particular" for "practical" is significant. The word "practical" is of course ambiguous and is susceptible of different interpretations. But it at once lends itself to the construction that "what is 'practical'" is "what affects our conduct in daily life," in the sense in which we distinguish a "practical man" or "man of affairs" from a "dreamer" or "scholar." In considering "practical[1]" consequences on this view, purposes and

[1] The fundamental ambiguity of the word "practical" comes out clearly in an illustration given by James (*Phil. Rev.* 1908. Reprinted in *Meaning of Truth*, p. 209). "When one says that a sick man has now practically recovered...one usually means just the opposite of practically in the literal sense. One means that, although untrue in strict practice, what one says is true in theory, true virtually, *certain to be* true."—But surely what is meant in such a case is just the reverse of what James says. It means, not that it *is true* that the man has recovered, but that for all practical purposes it *makes no difference* that he has not *quite* recovered, so that it can be said that he is "*practically* well." The

needs, i.e. practical interests will be brought to the front, and volition and emotion will have a large share in determining the value of a concept.

Such is the theory explicitly maintained in the " Will to Believe "; the passional nature is raised to the level of the intellectual nature as a determinant of truth.

For purposes of criticism it will be of use to consider just how this conclusion is reached. The problem may be stated: Required—A theory that will satisfy the emotional nature and ensure the satisfaction of its longings and aspirations. Solution: Raise the value of the emotional element, i.e. recognise the right of emotion to enter as a determining factor into the construction of truth. But a difficulty arises. When we believe, we *think* we believe independently of our emotions and will. However eloquently the "rights" of the passional nature may be stated, however certainly it may be proved that emotional interest does enter into the formation of our beliefs, we are not satisfied unless we are assured that these beliefs are not *only* desirable but *true*. That is, we want to feel that our desires not only do, but " lawfully may " determine our beliefs. A further step must, then, be taken— " What satisfies our needs *is* true," or, in other words, " what works is true."

Pragmatism has thus become a theory of the nature and meaning of truth, viz. that " truth is *one species of good*, and not, as is usually supposed, a category distinct from good, and co-ordinate with it. The true is the name of whatever proves itself to be good in the

whole force of the "practical" here is to deny the strict truth of the statement, whereas on James' theory it must be " true " because there is no *practical* difference in his conduct.

way of belief, and good, too, for definite assignable reasons[1]."

The fact that Pragmatism was formulated to ensure the recognition of the "rights" of our passional nature is brought out by Dr Schiller's definition of it as "a systematic protest against all ignoring of the purposiveness of actual knowing[2]," which, he points out, is through and through permeated by " interests, purposes, desires, choices, emotions, ends, goods, postulations." The "Spirit" of Pragmatism he describes as "a bigger thing which may fitly be denominated Humanism," and which may be summed up in the dictum *"Homo mensura."*

While, then, Pragmatism claims—wrongly it seems to me—that it is only a method compatible with any metaphysic (as witness the "corridor theory" of Papini), yet, Dr Schiller admits that it points definitely to *a* metaphysic of voluntaristic type. We thus reach his final definition of Pragmatism as "a conscious application to epistemology (or logic) of a teleological psychology, which implies, ultimately, a voluntaristic metaphysic[3]."

It is, however, as a theory of truth that Pragmatism will be mainly considered in the following study, for it is around the question of the nature of truth that the battle between pragmatism and absolutism is waged, and it is as supplying a criterion of truth that the pragmatist claims novelty for his doctrine.

The criterion that he offers seems to be essentially an outcome of the democratic principle to submit every question to the "poll of the people" and to cut the knot of every difficulty by the "counting of heads,"—or hearts !

---

[1] James, *Pragmatism*, p. 76.   [2] *Studies in Humanism*, p. 11.
[3] *Ibid*. p. 12.

It is on this account that Pragmatism has been described as characteristically "American." Dr Schiller has, however, on several occasions denied the "vulgar derivation of Pragmatism from the national American character"—a view that James' unfortunate expression "cash-value" to elucidate the ambiguous meaning of "practical consequences," and his frequent use of American commercial slang in explaining fundamental conceptions, did much to propagate, but which certainly cannot be maintained. Nevertheless, there can, I think, be not the least doubt that Pragmatism is penetrated through and through with the democratic spirit.

But when we turn to consider French Voluntarism we are in an entirely different atmosphere. Here the mark is of detachment from daily affairs and of concern with the innermost life of individual, personal experience; the philosopher looks away from "words" and "actions" to be "tête-à-tête avec sa propre pensée," as Bergson has said of Ravaisson, and which might be said with equal truth of Maine de Biran, the first French voluntarist, and of Bergson himself, the latest and most illustrious. Perhaps one of the strongest impressions left after reading *Les Données immédiates de la Conscience* is the vital distinction the author finds between the self of daily life—the self in which the plain man is predominantly interested—and the fundamental self which underlies the surface self so deeply that a vigorous effort of regressive analysis is necessary in order to penetrate to it—an effort of which the majority of men, including the pragmatists, are quite incapable. Only this fundamental self, however, pierces reality; the superficial self, because under the bondage of bodily requirements and social needs, is condemned to touch only the distorted surface of the real. It is true that Bergson protests that the self must not be regarded as "split up"; nevertheless the distinction established is radical and constitutes an irreconcilable dualism between the two selves.

The "regressive effort" demanded by Bergson is no less beyond the capacity of the plain man than is the vision of a mystic trance. There could not be a greater condemnation of social life, nor a more complete severance of it from all contact with the real. The ultimate reality may be "life," but it is not the commonplace life of ordinary men, the life into contact with which Pragmatism seeks to come and the needs of which it seeks to satisfy.

This is all the more striking because M. Bergson professes as the mainspring of his philosophy the recognition of the necessity of coming into closer contact with life, as opposed to the abstractions of absolutistic philosophies, and here he professes an affinity with James. In England and America as in France, he says, there is a movement to bring philosophy back to a consideration of those vital problems which interest humanity "toute entière" and to abandon the arid discussions of the Schools[1]. Of this movement James is the leader of English speaking peoples, Bergson of French.

Yet, surely their standpoints are radically different. While the pragmatist looks outward for the effects of theory on conduct, while he seeks what practical difference a given theory may make to us as social beings bound together by interest, love and action, Bergson looks downward to penetrate the reality that flows beneath the

[1] In lectures on "Nature of the Soul"—not yet published.

activities of daily life, and turns away from man as social being to man as individual, and from the standpoint of the real, he deplores the rare, and never complete, achievement of pure individuality.

This difference in outlook is fundamental. It is true that James lays stress on "temperament" and hence is led to emphasise individual differences—or idiosyncrasies—but he deals with men as individuals recognised as such *in* society and drawing their worth from the society of which they are essential elements. There is in James no trace of the view that in society "we 'are acted' rather than act ourselves" which sums up Bergson's final condemnation of social life from the metaphysical standpoint. If, then, both the American and the French philosopher treat of the "vital problems" which make philosophy "thick," nevertheless their treatment differs widely. Resemblances there are, indeed, between them, resemblances that spring from a common distrust of intellect, but—as we shall see— the distrust leads to diverse conclusions.

There is, however, a point of contact between James and Bergson arising from a non-pragmatic strain in the former due to his love for mystical experience, which, towards the end of his life and while he was greatly influenced by Bergson, seems to have overshadowed the pragmatic elements in his philosophy. Yet even here, in spite of his recognition of a mystical source of knowledge, James himself continued to base his own belief on pragmatic postulation. His leaning towards mysticism may be due, perhaps, to his desire to "open the way to all the winds that blow." But in their view of the nature of truth, hence of philosophic method, James and Bergson are diametrically opposed. We shall find that, in spite of superficial resemblances, the divergence of standpoint is fundamental.

Our purpose, then, is to shew, from a study of French Voluntarism, that, in the course of its development from Kant, while it exhibits in Renouvier an element, which, mingling with the "principle of Peirce," brings forth the pragmatism of William James, it nevertheless developes on independent and even antagonistic lines. On the one hand we find the main line of development in the spiritualistic philosophy of contingency derived from Maine de Biran and culminating in the anti-pragmatic intuitionism of Bergson and the "New Philosophy" of MM. Le Roy and Wilbois; on the other hand is the not less anti-pragmatic philosophy of "*Idées-forces*," which is opposed both to the moralism of Renouvier and to the intuitionism of Bergson.

II. THE NATURE OF FRENCH VOLUN-
TARISTIC PHILOSOPHY

In France, since the time of Descartes, there has been a close connection between philosophy and mathematics. The study of mathematics fostered the French love of "clearness," and gave rise to the philosophy of clear ideas which has predominated in France from Descartes till the end of the eighteenth century. The main assumption of Mathematical Rationalism is that Reality can be adequately attained by "clearness of conception" which provides sufficiency of evidence. The fundamental conceptions of philosophy being attained with maximum clearness, principles are given from which deductions can be made with mathematical certainty and precision.

But, as we have seen, the nineteenth century witnessed a strong reaction against this intellectualist philosophy with its logically inevitable outcome in determinism. The way for this reaction was prepared by the development of psychology as a subject of independent study, which led to the recognition of the volitional activity of mind as of equal—or even greater—significance with cognition. Emphasis on the active side of experience has dispelled the intellectualist view of mind as passive in its recognition of truth, and hence has led to the denial of "clearness" as an adequate criterion of certainty.

The result is *Voluntarism* in its various psychological, epistemological, and metaphysical forms. Its essential distinction from "Intellectualism" or "Rationalism" may be summed up briefly in that Voluntarism holds that psychologically, will is more fundamental than intellect; that metaphysically, the ultimate nature of reality is some form of will; finally, that in epistemology, will must be recognised as essential to the construction of truth; hence—while for the Intellectualist certainty is measured by clearness of intellectual apprehension, for the voluntarist certainty is greatest when will is most intense.

Further, the admission of will as a *real* factor carries with it the recognition of contingency in the Universe.

It has sometimes been asserted that Voluntarism goes back to Descartes, the claim being grounded upon Descartes' theory of judgment in which the will plays an important part that becomes especially prominent in his treatment of error. We shall, however, find, I think, that this assertion is not well founded.

Descartes adopts a twofold division of mind into "perception of the understanding" and "action of the will." The understanding is purely passive in perceiving or apprehending the ideas about which a judgment may be formed ; the will affirms or denies. Judgment is thus a product of will and understanding. The problem of certainty, that is of truth and error, arises with regard to judgments. Since the understanding is purely passive it is entirely determined from without, that is by God. How, then, can it err? The difficulty with which Descartes is faced is to avoid attributing error to God. It is for this purpose that he resorts to the will. The argument may be briefly stated as follows. Error is more than mere negation; it is defect. It must then arise from the understanding or the will. But it cannot arise from the understanding alone, since that is a faculty given by God, therefore its conceptions must be true.

The will, however, is indifferent to truth or error; it is also of much wider range than the understanding, hence it can deal with matters that are not understood and, because of its indifference, falls easily into error.

Thus error arises from the affirmation or denial of anything that is not clearly and distinctly conceived; that is, error is due to assent based on inadequate knowledge.

It would appear, then, that error can be rightly attributed to the will only in so far as the will does not restrain judgment within the limits of clear and distinct perception. On the other hand, wherever there is such clear and distinct perception the will assents, great clearness of the understanding being always succeeded by strong inclination in the will. Were the understanding as ample as the will, the perfection of both would be attained, and there could be no error, for "if I always clearly knew what was true and good, I should never have any difficulty in determining what judgment I ought to come to, and what choice I ought to make, and I should thus be entirely free without ever being indifferent[1]." Error, then, is due to the will.

In criticising this theory as a basis for Voluntarism we must remember: that the first principle is given by understanding alone, viz. by clear and distinct perception; that what is *clearly perceived must* be assented to by the will ("the nature of my mind is such as to compel me to

[1] Med. IV. Veitch's Edition, p. 138. (Haldane and Ross, vol. I. p. 175.)

assent to what I clearly conceive while I so conceive it "); hence, human will does not create truth but finds it ready made in clear perception and assents to it. At best the will constitutes error only, not truth. Moreover, Descartes asserts that knowledge of the understanding *ought* always to precede judgment of the will.

It appears obvious, then, that the will is only brought in to account for error. Furthermore, Descartes considers that indifference in the will is a defect, due to inadequate knowledge. This is brought out more strongly by Malebranche—who in many points was a more consistent Cartesian than Descartes—for he asserts that the will is always inclined towards truth and good in general, hence is determined by good, and errs only by deflection in a special direction which the mind fails, because of inadequate knowledge, to recognise as not good. (By what criterion the " good " is to be judged we are not told.)

Finally, it is in thought that Descartes finds the essence of mind. The fact that his theory of error necessitates the admission of will as on a par with thought—an admission that is fatal to his rationalism—shows that it is an after thought. Again in Malebranche we find greater consistency coupled with even greater failure to account for error. He relates will to mind as motion is related to matter; will is not, therefore, the essence of mind, and he adds, " I do not think that it would be possible to conceive a mind which does not think, although it may be very easy to conceive one which does not feel, which does not imagine, and even which does not will," hence, " all these modifications are not essential to it. Thought quite alone is the essence of mind."

[1] *Recherche*, III. Pt. I. 1.

It is this that is essential to Descartes' whole theory of evidence and which expresses his fundamental thought.

We conclude then that Voluntarism cannot legitimately be traced back to Descartes. That there is an appearance of voluntarism in his admission that error involves choice on our part may be granted. But my contention is that that admission was not made in the sense in which Pragmatism affirms it, but for the sole purpose of exonerating God from the charge of causing error in us. The difference is essential in that Descartes sets over against the mind the truths which the mind clearly and distinctly perceives, and whose truth is determined by clearness and distinctness of perception and *not* by the inclination of the will which accompanies clear perception.

The fact that he so utterly failed in his attempt satisfactorily to account for error by attributing it to human will is but another proof that his treatment differs widely from that of the pragmatists, and that he is far from admitting the existence of " man-made " truths.

It is a significant fact that—with the sole exception of Renouvier—the question of error does not engage the attention of French Voluntarists, whereas it is the prominent feature of Pragmatism, the *raison d'être* of which is to supply a theory of knowledge that will account for the fact of error and provide a criterion by which we may distinguish the true from the false, for, says Dr Schiller, " let no man imagine that he has a theory of Truth unless it *does* distinguish True from False[1]."

Pragmatism, it must be remembered, has sprung from reaction against intellectualistic Absolutism, and is both

[1] *Proc. Arist. Soc.* N.S. xi. p. 145.

a protest against the exclusion of will and emotion—
" human purposes "—from the theory of knowledge and
an attempt to extend the "working hypothesis" of science
to all departments of thought, hence to define " truth " as
successful working.

Whereas Pragmatism is of epistemological origin,
French Voluntarism has sprung from the psychological
consideration of the *fact of activity* itself, emphasis on
which has become so characteristic of modern thought.

Insistence upon the predominantly volitional character
of experience does not in any way necessitate a pragmatic
epistemology and, as we shall see, the spiritualistic voluntarism developed from de Biran has more affinity with
the voluntarism of Schopenhauer than with the "practical
reason" of Kant. It would perhaps be most fitly denominated " Activism "—to employ, in a slightly different
sense, a word used by Eucken to distinguish his voluntarism
from pragmatism[1].

1. SPIRITUALISTIC ACTIVISM.

(1) From the time of Maine de Biran, who may be
regarded as the founder of French Voluntarism, stress has
been laid upon the consciousness of personal activity,
which, in its immediacy affords a basis for philosophy
and points to the adoption of the standpoint of personal
experience as fundamental.

[1] Cf. " Pragmatism which has lately made such headway, especially
among English-speaking peoples, is more inclined to fashion the world
and life in accordance with human conditions and human needs, than to
invest spiritual activity with independence in relation to these, and to
apply its standards to the testing and sifting of the whole content of
our human life." (Eucken, *Grundlinien einer neuenlebensanschauung*,
p. 312.)

The first step in this direction was taken by de Biran when he sought for a more inward point of view than that adopted by the sensationalism of Condillac and the Ideologists. This central experience he found in the "immediate apperception" of self-activity, and upon this, as the primary fact of consciousness, his whole philosophy is based. It is in the immediate experience of the self as causal agent that de Biran finds the true meaning of "cogito ergo sum." Accordingly he considers that the Cartesian formula must be re-interpreted in order to reduce it to its "true psychological expression; I feel or perceive myself free cause, then I am really cause[1]." In thus substituting "*Volo*" for "*Cogito*" de Biran appears clearly in opposition to the Rationalism of Descartes as well as to the Sensationalism of Condillac. While Descartes perceived that the affirmation of thought implies the reality of the subject which thinks, he stopped short at the self as thinking subject, hence was unable to reach the self as person; whereas it is the sentiment of personality that animates the doctrine of de Biran, and enables him to claim that "'I am an acting force' has all the value and the infallible certainty of a principle[2]."

The immediate consciousness of self-activity in which de Biran finds the central point of psychology, the basis of consciousness and the foundation of all knowledge is action willed in opposition to a resistance in the over-coming of which force is exerted. It is this "acting force which we call will"—or effort which is the primary fact

[1] Nouvelles considérations sur les rapports du physique et du moral de l'homme. p. 249.
[2] *Oeuv. phil.* III. p. 22.

of consciousness. Further, "The self identifies itself completely with this acting force. But the existence of the force is a fact for the *self* only so far as it is exerted, and it is exerted only so far as it can apply itself to a resisting or inert term. The force is then determined or actualised only in the relation to its term of application, moreover the latter is determined as resisting or inert only in relation to the actual force which moves it, or tends to impress movement on it[1]." There is, then, an essential duality; effort is a relation between a force and a limit to the force ; the *cause* of the effort " becomes *self* by the sole fact of the distinction which is established between the subject of this free effort, and the term which resists immediately by its own inertia[2]." Consciousness of effort gives, on the one hand, the self known through its willing, on the other, the not-self known through the resistance with which the self meets.

This derivation, however, appears to presuppose the distinction of self and not-self for which it is to account. Although, undoubtedly, the resistance encountered by the will would aid in the development of mind in its relation to external reality, it is insufficient to account for the origin of the distinction. In other words, it has yet to be proved that the consciousness of effort *is* the primordial fact of consciousness. It would appear rather that experience of effort involves some rudimentary conception of self, hence some rudimentary conception of not-self to account for resistance. De Biran's explanation remains then ideological and not properly genetic.

Moreover, under the conception of "effort" de Biran confuses "mental effort" or activity of will, and "muscular

---

[1] *Oeuv. Inéd.* I. p. 47.   [2] *Ibid.* p. 48.

effort" or sensation. He nowhere makes clear what exactly he means by the force that is one term—or limit—of effort. This omission is pointed out by E. Naville, the editor of de Biran's later works, and he suggests that "it is necessary, in order to enter into the views of the author, to leave out any objective notion or representation of the movement considered in external space, the fact of the inner sense not being able to contain an element of this order[1]."

Certainly such a deduction is necessary, but it seems to me that, according to de Biran's view, it is not possible, for resistance is an indispensable factor in the effort that is the primary fact of inner experience; the movement *willed* requires, as its correlative, resistance to the movement. The condition of volitional activity is thus the existence of something given outside consciousness. Will may, then, be the primary fact of consciousness, but it is not ontologically ultimate.

There is indeed an ambiguity apparent in his conception of "activity." In combining with it as an essential constituent the notion of resistance, it would appear to be of the nature of what is now called *conation*. But the activity of which we are immediately aware is an activity of knowing no less than of willing, hence it cannot be identified with conation rather than with cognition. There is, then, no justification for regarding activity in the sense of volitional activity as more fundamental than cognitive activity, that is, as *psychologically* ultimate.

Further, de Biran's view of will as essentially bound up with voluntary *movement*[2] is unduly restricted. This

---

[1] *Oeuv. Ined.* ii. p. 412.

[2] e.g. "One can conceive a sentient being, inwardly organised as we

is indeed the cause of his confusion in dealing with the conception of effort, and prevents the amendment suggested by Naville.

De Biran, then, rests philosophy upon a psychological basis—the immediate experience of personal activity, that is, the consciousness of the self as a causal agent—and from this standpoint he obtains a psychological deduction of the categories. In the perception by the self of its self as a cause de Biran finds the type of all ideas of power, force, causality; thus effort is *one*, hence the category of *unity*; the self is *cause*, hence the category of *causality*.

In seeking a metaphysical reality empirically given, de Biran endeavoured to steer a middle way between empiricism and the ontology of Descartes. But in taking as his basis the subjective psychological fact of will he was forced to remain at the point of view of empiricism, hence he failed to explain the universality and necessity of the categories he deduced therefrom.

Nevertheless, his insistence upon the supreme importance of the fact of activity led König to style him the "French Kant," for, he says, "Denselben Begriff der Spontaneität, durch welchen Kant die empiristische Erkenntnisslehre reformirte, führt Biran in der sensualistischen Psychologie ein ; was dort erkenntnisstheoretische Hypothese ist, wird uns hier als psychologische Thatsache aufgewiesen ; als Gegenstück zur transscendentalen Function des Verstandes tritt uns die empirische Activität des psychologischen Subjects entgegen[1]."

are but devoid of mobility, this being would experience needs, vague desires, but *his will* could not be born."

(*Influence de l'Habitude*, p. 111 n. Italics are de Biran's.)

[1] *Philosophische Monatshefte*, Vol. xxv. p. 169. "The same idea of

But König fails to recognise the essential difference in their use of the concept of activity. The significance of Kant consists not merely in his emphasis on the activity of mind in opposition to the empiricists, but in his showing that the activity which expresses the nature of mind is universal and objective. But de Biran, owing to his standpoint, which, in spite of himself, remained purely empirical, was, as we have seen, unable to explain the universality and necessity of the categories. The pure concepts of the understanding cannot be obtained by a purely psychological deduction. For de Biran the activity of mind as expressed in will, or the fact of effort, is but one element of mind, and the self, which he identifies with effort, is thus one element abstracted from consciousness, and is a special fact to be verified by introspection, instead of being, as with Kant, the total subjective side of a unitary experience. De Biran's error is due to his entire neglect of the part played by understanding. To describe him as the "French Kant" seems to me, then, a great exaggeration; he might with more reason be styled "the French Schopenhauer."

The importance of the fact of activity de Biran recognised early, and while still a professed disciple of Condillac he wrote in his *Journal Intime*—"It is much to be desired that a man skilled in introspection should analyse the will as Condillac has analysed the understanding[1]." It is true that the sensationalist Destutt de Tracy, a zealous adherent

spontaneity by means of which Kant reformed empirical epistemology Biran introduced into the sensationalistic psychology. What was there an epistemological hypothesis is shewn to us here as a psychological fact; the empirical activity of the psychological subject appears as the counterpart of the transcendental function of the understanding."

[1] *Pensées*, ed. Naville, p. 123.

of Condillac, had recognised that will is essential for the development of the self and the perception of external reality, but he remained at the Condillacian standpoint, and hence failed to realise the consequences of this admission of an original active element in experience; it was left to de Biran to develope the implications of the fact of activity as experienced in the consciousness of personal effort.

In the process of that development, in spite of some ambiguities and with no clear consciousness of the full import of the standpoint he had adopted, de Biran laid the foundations of that " Psychology of first causes "—to adopt a name employed by Dr Boyce Gibson[1]—which, from the inner point of view of the experient, perceives the self as free cause[2]. From this point of view the conception of freedom becomes fundamental.

(2) The essential conception of de Biran's philosophy —that in the immediate consciousness of self-activity we attain the real—bears not a little resemblance to the main theme of Schelling, and in Ravaisson we find a combination of the metaphysics of the latter with the philosophical psychology of the former. The confluence of the two streams of thought is due rather to an essential similarity than to the more or less accidental meeting of Ravaisson and Schelling at Munich. Certainly the influence of Schelling is pronounced throughout the period we are considering in which we find a curious mingling of

[1] *Personal Idealism*—" The Problem of Freedom."

[2] This view has recently received confirmation in a paper read by Dr Boyce Gibson before the Aristotelian Society in January 1912. He here explicitly refers to Maine de Biran as inaugurating the "psychology of the self as a free first cause." In the earlier essay, although no reference was made to de Biran, his influence is apparent.

profound respect for, and belief in the progress of, modern Science with a romantic impulse to seek truth in a formless intuition and rely, in the last resort, on mystical symbolism.

These tendencies are well marked in Felix Ravaisson, who, although by no means a prolific writer and little known outside France, has nevertheless exerted a profound influence on the current of French philosophy, which, as he foretold, is setting in the direction of a spiritualistic dynamism, which recognises that "matter is only the last degree and as it were the shadow of existence; that the most real existence, of which every other is but an imperfect sketch, is that of the soul; that, in reality to be is to live, and to live is to think and to will; that nothing is made in ultimate analysis, save by moral effort; that good, beauty alone are sufficient to explain the universe and its author; that the infinite and the absolute, which nature presents only imperfectly, consist in spiritual liberty; that liberty is thus the ultimate foundation of things, and that, beneath the unrest and strife that ruffle the surface upon which phenomena take place, in the depths in the essential and eternal truth, all is beauty, love and harmony[1]."

I have quoted this passage at length because it admirably sums up Ravaisson's attitude, an attitude that has permeated French philosophy until its culmination in Bergson who is as much an artist as a metaphysician, and sums up that philosophy which, addressing itself "to feeling as much as to reason," explains the inert by the living, and reconciles "in an harmony sensible to the heart, terms perhaps irreconcilable for intelligence[2]."

---

[1] *La Phil. en France*, p. 285 (2nd Edition).

[2] Bergson on Ravaisson in *Acad. des Sc.* 1907, p. 43.

This philosophy was virtually contained in Ravaisson's first work, *De l'Habitude*—(published in 1833)—which considered the question whether the existence of matter can be reconciled with a philosophy that derives from consciousness the first principle of being in general. In the phenomena of habit we see will passing into automatism, hence may not nature be "a will fallen asleep," and mechanism but the fossilised residue of a spiritual activity? Since, in contracting a habit the free acts of mind approach ever nearer the mechanical movements of matter, we are led to observe a similarity between them, and to conclude that by habit mind, or consciousness, is degraded into mechanical movement or matter.

Habit is necessarily the work of a being endowed with a true identity, capable of modification and originally free. The identity essential for the formation of habit is given by consciousness of will or effort in which the self is directly revealed under the form of voluntary activity. This conception Ravaisson directly refers to the influence of de Biran. There is, however, an important development in Ravaisson's treatment, in that he makes habit the link between mind and matter, the mean term between will and nature. Between habit and instinct there is a difference of degree only. All movement presupposes desire, or tendency; instinct is natural tendency, habit is acquired tendency, the result of a universally operative law by virtue of which all being tends to persist in any state into which it comes. Thus habit arises, and leads to degradation from the completed unity of personality to the extreme diffusion of impersonality. The vital distinction between the organic and the inorganic is to be found, moreover, in their different relation to time. Life implies duration, hence the identity that is essential to personality; the inorganic has no definite relation with time, hence it is impersonal, diffused, lacking in true identity.

In his doctrine of the Ego, also, Ravaisson developes and carries further de Biran's views. He does not regard effort as a self-sufficient explanation. External resistance is replaced by desire. Effort presupposes a desire which is based on the feeling of union with a necessary Being, which union is incomplete. In substituting desire for external resistance as the other term of effort, Ravaisson attempts to dispense with the non-ego. In basing desire on the feeling of union with a necessary Being the non-ego reappears as a final cause—"the attraction of the ideal"—to use Boutroux's phrase. Finality is thus the hidden spring of mechanism. This replacement of the efficient by the final cause—that is the subordination of mechanism to finality—is characteristic of this phase of spiritualistic philosophy that has for its essential basis the conception of freedom.

(3) But, it may be asked, is not determinism essential to the conception and progress of positive science?

It was with the purpose of answering this question in the negative that M. Boutroux—in his now famous doctoral thesis—examined the notion of contingency as related to the determinism upon which science is based. The view put forward in this work—*De la Contingence des Lois de la Nature*, published in 1875—was further developed and illustrated in a course of lectures, delivered at the Sorbonne in 1892-3, on "L'Idée de Loi Naturelle," the purpose of which was to examine the laws found in the sciences with a view to determining their nature, objectivity and significance.

These two small, but extremely important works, constitute the chief part of M. Boutroux's philosophical writings. There are two main points: (a) There is a real discontinuity between the sciences; it is impossible to pass deductively from one to the other since each includes a new element not found in the preceding. The superior forms of being are irreducible to the lower, hence cannot be bound to them by a necessary bond. (b) "Necessity" and "determination" are not the same thing, and in admitting the latter we exclude the former. The first of these points is examined more fully in the earlier work, the second in the latter, but they are intimately connected, the purpose being to show that science does not require a rigorous determinism—or necessity—hence does not contradict the notions of individuality, finality and freedom, upon which our moral belief rests. The problem is, then, to consider "up to what point the laws which rule phenomena participate in necessity[1]." If contingency is only another name for ignorance, then necessity rules, but, "if it should happen that the given world should manifest a certain amount of ultimately irreducible contingency," then, "there would be room to think that the laws of nature are not sufficient by themselves and have their ground in the causes which dominate them: in such manner that the point of view of understanding would not be the final point of view of the knowledge of them."

Cause and effect is the only perfect type of necessity[2], hence the scientific ideal is, M. Boutroux holds, to reduce

---

[1] *C.L.N.* p. 5.

[2] Boutroux's conception of cause and effect as the perfect type of necessity, in that it is ultimately reducible to an analytic relation, is

all laws to particular cases of one supreme law of causal synthesis. This, by reason of the radical discontinuity between the stages of being represented by the different sciences, is, he concludes, impossible.

M. Boutroux starts with the widest conception of the given, namely, " being " or " the *fact* pure and simple, still undetermined," and asserts that as such it is a contingent form of the possible, hence contains, as actual, an element not contained in the merely possible, for it implies the realisation of *one possible* in preference to another. He then proceeds to show that the modes of being are contingent, and not capable of being derived analytically once being is posited. Thus, throughout the scale—matter, bodies, living bodies, man—each new stage involves a new element irreducible to the lower: hence the higher cannot be deduced from the lower—or less developed—because the higher involves an additional and incalculable factor. Thus " there is not equivalence, relation of pure and simple causality, between a man and the elements that have given him birth, between the developed being and the being in process of formation[1]." It is not possible, then, to bind the superior forms of beings to the inferior by a necessary bond. Necessity implies deduction, or the relation of antecedent to consequent, and is not an equivalent of determination. This opposition of " necessity" and " determinism" is the foundation of Boutroux's doctrine of contingency. It is most clearly formulated in his discussion of physical laws. " One must be careful, in

obviously opposed to the conception of cause in Inductive Logic, such as that of J. S. Mill. According to Boutroux's classification, Mill's treatment of causation would fall under the head of " determinism."

[1] *C.L.N.* p. 28.

fact," he says, "not to confuse determinism and necessity: necessity expresses the impossibility that a thing should be other than it is; determinism expresses the totality of conditions which ensure that the phenomenon must be such as it is, with all its properties[1]." A necessary law must then be abstract, such as the law of conservation of energy. A law which should regulate the distribution of force would be properly a determining law, but such a law will be purely experimental, hence not necessitating. Determining laws, if they are also to express necessity, must be capable of reduction to abstract logical formulation. But in the case of experimental laws this is not possible. Hence we are faced by the dilemma: "Either necessity without determinism, or determinism without necessity[2]."

The importance of this distinction lies in the fact that the denial of necessity no longer involves the destruction of positive science, but rather renders such science possible. Science seeks facts to build up laws; it does not impose the laws on the facts. Laws are only "the bed where flows the torrent of facts; they have cut it out, although they follow it[3]." Laws, then, have no *constraining force*; they are determining in so far as they express prevision of facts. Science, therefore, remains valid and applicable without affording any ground for belief in necessity.

It is not easy to determine precisely what M. Boutroux understands by a "fact," nor how far he would seem to admit a "brute fact" from which the scientific fact is elaborated, nor what is the relation of this fact to the real. In his latest work—*Science and Religion*—M. Boutroux declares that the aim of science is twofold: to obtain

[1] *L'Idée...*, p. 58.　　　[2] *Ibid.* p. 59.　　　[3] *C.L.N.* p. 39.

positive knowledge of nature, and to influence nature. In pursuit of the latter purpose, science formulates laws by "inferring them from the simple facts[1]." The fact itself is "constructed by the mutual action and reaction of mind and of knowledge," and in the same way, he conjectures, "facts themselves are capable, through elaboration, of becoming laws." But there is surely a difficulty here. How, in the first place, is the mind to obtain knowledge of the "simple fact" if it be confined to interaction on its own knowledge by means of which it constructs a "scientific fact" that is admittedly *not* the "simple fact," for, M. Boutroux asks, "is not the scientific fact itself... already a constructed symbol, an imaginary objective equivalent of the original fact[2]?" Do we, then, ever know the original fact at all, and, if not, how can it be said that science seeks "to know being in itself and the permanent substance of things[3]?" It appears then as if science in the pursuit of its second aim—the influencing of nature—were compelled to forego the first to obtain positive knowledge of nature, for "science consists in substituting for things, symbols which express a certain aspect of them—the aspect that can be denoted by relatively precise relations, intelligible and available for all men[4]." Yet, as M. Boutroux points out—"the expression must, necessarily, preserve a relation to the thing expressed; otherwise it would be worthless[5]." How, then, we may ask, can it be contended that the necessity lies only in the symbolic representation of science, and not in the nature of things themselves? It seems to me that there is a real dilemma here. Either the necessity we

---

[1] *Op. cit.* (Eng. Tr.), p. 355.   [2] *Ibid.* p. 356.   [3] *Ibid.* p. 355.
[4] *Ibid.* p. 361.   [5] *Ibid.* p. 362.

seem to find in scientific laws is inherent in the nature of things, or it is due to a manipulation of "facts" by the scientific mind and corresponds to no *real* aspect of nature. But in that case, surely it is at least odd that such manipulation should enable us to control the course of things. There must be, it would seem, an underlying necessity that we *find* in things, and not merely an order that we *impose* on them for purposes of scientific control. Presumably, M. Boutroux would reply by insisting on his distinction between necessity and determinism. But this does not seem to me to meet the objection that the determinism upon which science is based is a characteristic inherent in the facts themselves and not a mere regulative device of mind. We are forced to admit, either that scientific laws are merely an ingenious device corresponding to nothing in the nature of things, or that they express a determination inherent in nature itself, hence a *necessary* determination. In the first case it is inexplicable that science should render possible the prevision of facts; in the second, it becomes impossible to get rid of necessity, not as an outside compelling force coercing reluctant facts —a travesty of the notion of necessity that surely needs no refutation—but as an inherent necessity that makes *radical contingency* inconceivable.

We conclude, then, that the distinction between necessity and determinism is not enough to ensure the admission of contingency into the universe of being. As has been already pointed out, it is the attempt to save the determinism postulated by science that led M. Boutroux to make this distinction, and to end in a dualism which sets on one side inchoate facts, and on the other in-determined mind which imposes determination on the facts.

But in the conclusions that M. Boutroux draws from the recognition of contingency, there is an indication of another point of view from which it may be possible to vindicate the reality of contingency while at the same time justifying the existence of science.

Starting from the conception of contingency as essentially involving the efficiency of free activity—such activity being of fundamentally the same nature as human causal agency—we may be led to recognise that this activity which finds its highest empirical manifestation in human liberty, is yet also present in some degree in every grade of being. The problem will then be to account for the uniformity of "natural laws" which seems to set them in a realm apart from that of free initiative, though sharing in the same fundamentally voluntaristic nature.

Even in human activity we find a tendency to form "habits," to run along a groove of fixed activity, so that habit becomes "second nature" partaking of the automatism of a machine. But, if in the highest scale of being we thus find free activity tending to fall into ruts, we should expect to find this tendency more and more accentuated as we descend this scale, until, in the inferior grades of being, "habits" are expressed by "laws of nature" which seem to be the complete denial of freedom, whereas they are the result of an exercise of free activity that has become stereotyped. For human purposes it is convenient to accept these laws as fixed—as based on physical necessity and not on spontaneity. From the point of view of science we may accept a determinism that is the result of stereotyped activity. From the epistemological point of view, however, "what we call laws of nature is the totality of the methods that we have found to adapt things to our intelligence and to bend them to the accomplishment of our wills[1]." Thus laws of nature express only our way of considering things, not their real manner of being.

In thus recognising in all grades of being a principle, the highest manifestation of which is liberty, the doctrine of contingency is seen to possess a practical as well as a theoretical interest, since, not only does it allow to man a real efficacy in action—an activity in more than name— but it leads him to recognise that being in none of its grades is known "right to its foundation[2]" by the positive sciences for "it has yet to be known in its creative source." This creative source, the end and pattern of all activity, is the supremely free Being—God. We are thus led to a reformulation of the cosmological argument. If action is to be real, if necessity is to be banished from the universe, then there must be a limit to the series of causes, and that limit must be the highest and supreme Being, God, the creator of all being. It would seem that we are thereby led back to a necessary series again, hence to the conception of necessity, and Boutroux admits that this is so, only that it is necessity under a new form, that of *duty*, which is a constraining force not from the speculative but from the practical point of view, since it is an end which in itself *merits* realisation, hence is the necessity of moral obligation and is not of a physical nature. It is only because activity is free that the end, as duty, can be realised.

It is important to remember that necessity in its new form is not a speculative concept; were we limited to the

[1] Cf. p. 25 supra. *L'Idée...*, p. 143.
[2] *C.L.N.* p. 140.

speculative point of view we should be forced to stop short of the desired end, but we are not merely speculative but essentially active beings, and in every action we have the consciousness of liberty as an infinite power which carries us beyond ourselves to an infinite Being—actual perfection—which "is necessary with a practical necessity, that is, is absolutely worthy of being realised[1]."

The way in which M. Boutroux then attempts to reconcile permanence and change is interesting. The Supreme Being, the source of all activity, is Himself actual perfection, hence any change would involve degradation; the Supreme Being, therefore, is immutable. On the other hand, throughout the scale of being there is an increasing divergence from the perfection attained only in the highest; hence it is only by change that the Ideal can be attained. In this way the reality of progress is asserted. Nor is progress confined to man; all beings feel the attraction of the Infinite, hence are called to the Ideal by virtue of the possession of that activity which is at once an indispensable condition and a spur to its realisation.

The idea of "necessity" thus becomes "the translation, into logical language as abstract as possible, of the activity exerted by the ideal of things, by God on His creatures[2]." In so far as the ideal were completely attained, laws of nature would disappear to be replaced "by the free spring of willing beings towards perfection, by the free hierarchy of souls."

The conclusion seems to be, then, that contingency in the natural world can only be explained by the conception of a Creator or Supreme Being in whom supreme necessity is supreme liberty. In explaining the connection between

[1] *C.L.N.* p. 157.   [2] *Ibid.* p. 169.

the grades of being and filling up the lacunae left by the admission of contingency, it seems to me that M. Boutroux has destroyed, from the speculative point of view, the contingency he sought to establish.

The reaction against mechanistic materialism is the characteristic of present philosophy and the dominating note of French Voluntarism. The progress of the physical sciences encouraged the view that the world was all of one piece and could be understood on the mechanical pattern by reducing the higher to the lower and by making mind the shadow of matter.

An opposite tendency has now set in; the fundamental unity of the world is not denied, but rather insisted upon for the purpose of showing its spiritual affinity with man. By reversion to the Leibnizian conception of matter as momentary mind, the lower is brought into relation with the higher; there is a levelling up instead of a levelling down. Mind suffices to explain all; matter is the shadow of mind.

We may sum up this development in the words of a younger contemporary and ardent disciple of Ravaisson, M. Lachelier, who closes his work *Du fondement de l'Induction* with the reflection—"thus the realm of final causes, penetrating without destroying that of efficient causes, substitutes everywhere force for inertia, life for death and liberty for fatalism."

(4) These words may not ineptly be applied to the philosophy of M. Bergson the purpose of which—whether we can hold that it be attained or not—is to substitute " force for inertia, life for death and freedom for fatality."

In the philosophy of creative evolution we see the continuation of the current of French thought that

3—2

proceeds from Maine de Biran through Ravaisson and Boutroux. It would perhaps be hardly necessary to point out this—for no philosopher springs from the void —were it not that, to the English-speaking world at least, Bergson's views came with such force of novelty that he seemed to have no roots in the past, so that James declared " I have to confess that Bergson's originality is so profuse that many of his ideas baffle me entirely [1]." But just as the slow slipping of the loosened surface beneath a tilted rock causes it to rush down into the valley below if but a single stone be removed, so the slow accumulation of ideas results in the gradual formation of a new way of looking at the whole and transforms it suddenly and completely. To account for the fall of the rock we must take into consideration the whole process of gradual movement; to account for the transformation of a whole realm of thought we must look back to the current from which it proceeds. When we do this in the case of M. Bergson we find that he falls into place in the movement of French philosophy that we have designated Spiritualistic Activism. This is not to deny that his philosophy is essentially the work of an independent and original thinker whose development of the work of his predecessors bears the impress of an unusual individuality.

The distinguishing characteristic of M. Bergson's procedure is that he seeks to found a *positive* metaphysic, that is to say a metaphysic susceptible of continuous and indefinite progress. While admitting the relative independence of psychology and metaphysics he holds that each can set problems to the other and aid in their solution.

[1] *A Pluralistic Universe*, p. 226.

This procedure M. Bergson has himself illustrated with regard to the problem of the relation between mind and body, hence of the "existence and essence of matter." It is one of his most original achievements thus to have transposed a "cardinal metaphysical problem" into the psychological question—"Is memory a function of the brain." It is M. Bergson's hope that individual "systems" of philosophy will be gradually replaced by a true philosophy of evolution, itself an evolving whole, to be "built up by the collective and progressive effort of many thinkers, of many observers also, completing, correcting and improving one another[1]." Such a philosophy will be the slow work of time, and M.. Bergson himself claims only to define the method and indicate the possibility of its application, but it is a complete theory of the evolu tion of life that he offers us. His philosophy is thus primarily a metaphysic. He holds that theory of knowledge and theory of life are inseparable and certainly his own theory of knowledge is directly the result of his theory of reality. We may note, in passing, that such a view is diametrically opposed to the "Corridor Theory" of the pragmatist.

Unlike James and other pragmatists, then, M. Bergson does not begin with a discussion of the nature of truth— nowhere indeed does he directly face this question—but he begins by suggesting a theory of life that will be found to involve a peculiar view of the nature of knowledge. The problem of knowledge arises for him out of a consideration of the nature of reality. This is not strange since M. Bergson holds that previous philosophers have erred by reason of a mistaken view as to the nature of

[1] *Ev. Cr.* p. vii (E. Tr. p. xiv).

that reality which we directly apprehend. It is the common fault of philosophers, he says, to have believed that "by our senses and our consciousness, working as they ordinarily work, we should really perceive change in things and in ourselves[1]," and, since it is not to be denied that we are thereby landed in insoluble antinomies, they have concluded that contradiction is inherent in change itself.

M. Bergson reverses this. It is not change we apprehend but immobility; the reality is change, but we apprehend only that which does not change; the reality is time itself, a continuous flux, but we apprehend only its spatial representation. Hence we fall into contradiction. To avoid it, however, " there is no need to get away from time (we are only too far from it), there is no need to free ourselves from change (we are only too free from it), it would be necessary, on the contrary, to make an effort to seize again change and duration in their original mobility[2]."

The conception of duration, then, is fundamental and contains implicitly all that is essential to M. Bergson's philosophy. He claims moreover that duration is an immediate datum of consciousness. "Pure duration," he says, "is the form which the succession of our conscious states assumes when our ego lets itself *live*, when it refrains from separating its present state from its former states[3]." "*La durée*," then, is not what we ordinarily mean by time, nor is it what we ordinarily mean by duration ; for time, as usually conceived, is, M. Bergson contends, really one-dimensional space, and duration is commonly held to involve *something* that endures—

---

[1] *P.C.* p. 17. [2] *Ibid.* p. 14.
[3] *D.I.C.* p. 76 (E. Tr. p. 100).

a permanent in the midst of change and, therefore, opposed to change, not, M. Bergson holds, identical with it.

Characteristically M. Bergson does not start with the conception of duration but derives it as preliminary to a discussion of the problem of free will. From an analysis of the psychical nature of the self, M. Bergson concludes that there are two forms of multiplicity, radically ·diverse, to which correspond two forms of the self, one of which is free, the other determined. There is, on the one hand, "a self with well-defined states"—a self whose conscious states are set side by side along a time-line that is really space; on the other hand, there is "a self where succession implies fusion and organisation," a self whose states are not distinct and separate but continually interpenetrate and intermingle like the notes of a melody. The latter is the fundamental self, while the former is superficial since it is the shadow of the fundamental self "projected into space" and thereby losing the essential characteristic of living reality, its qualitative multiplicity.

In *Matière et Mémoire* the conception of duration is used to explain the relation between mind and matter which is a relation to be expressed in terms of time, not of space. That is, the difference between mind and matter is a difference between rhythms of duration. Mind is essentially memory, that is, the power of condensing an enormous multiplicity of vibrations which, spread out and infinitely diluted, constitute matter. Whereas mind, as pure memory, retains the past, matter is, as it were, "created anew" every instant; it is momentary mind.

Finally, in *L'Evolution Créatrice* duration becomes the "*élan vital*," a life impetus, the creative activity that is reality itself. Matter is now conceived not as infinitely diluted movement but as "inverse movement," the descending stream which falls back and interrupts the ascending movement of life.

The pronounced dualism of M. Bergson's earlier works has surely here given way to a monistic tendency. There is one movement, one vital impulse, one creative activity— "a reality which is making itself across a reality which is unmaking itself[1]." Reality is thus conceived as "incessant life, action, freedom." But while life is a movement, materiality is the inverse movement, and the one runs counter to the other. The ascending movement, the "*élan de vie*," is the continuous elaboration of the absolutely new, but it meets with an obstacle in matter, which is the inverse movement, and thus it cannot create absolutely. Life, then, bears in itself the obstacle to its onward progress, an obstacle that must, from the nature of the case, be ever increasing as life progresses. The final triumph of the life-impetus, to which undoubtedly M. Bergson looks, is thus, it would seem, rendered impossible, for life has always an ever-growing obstacle to surmount. The metaphors that are abundantly used to elucidate this extremely involved conception serve rather to obscure than to aid in its comprehension. For our present purpose, however, a detailed examination of the difficulties and contradictions thereby incurred is not necessary. The important point to note is that the reality that is making itself is essentially a psychical force, a spiritual activity that "we experience in ourselves when we act freely," and that it is identified with duration which is the very stuff of reality. Duration, which M. Bergson has defined as "the continuous progress of the past which gnaws into

[1] *Ev. Cr.* p. 269 (E. Tr. p. 261).

the future swelling as it advances[1]," describes the nature of spirit. In his Birmingham lecture M. Bergson very definitely recognises that the "life-impetus" is a spiritual force, that is, a force that "ever seeks to transcend itself, to extract from itself more than there is—in a word to create" and he adds, "a force which draws from itself more than it contains, which gives more than it has, is precisely what is called a *spiritual force*: in fact, I do not see how otherwise spirit is to be defined[2]." For M. Bergson, therefore, reality is spiritual existence, and "to exist is to change, to change is to mature, to mature is to go on creating oneself endlessly[3]."

Change, movement, activity, then, so far from being illusions in a world of non-being as the Eleatics held, express the ultimate nature of reality, for reality is continuous becoming, a "*devenir réel.*"

Why, then, do we so misrepresent the real? The answer according to M. Bergson is that our intellect has a purely practical function; it has been fashioned in the course of evolution in the interests of action. The conclusion that M. Bergson draws from his study of perception is that "the orientation of our consciousness towards action appears to be the fundamental law of our psychical life[4]." A very brief sketch of his theory of perception is here necessary, for it is of fundamental importance in estimating the part played by action in M. Bergson's philosophy.

There is a postulate, M. Bergson says, common to Realism and Idealism, viz. that "perception has a wholly speculative interest; it is pure knowledge." It is this that M. Bergson contests; perception is not speculative

---

[1] *Ev. Cr.* p. 5.
[2] *Hibbert Journal*, x. p. 40.
[3] *Ev. Cr.* p. 8 (E. Tr. p. 8).
[4] *M. et M.* p. 198 (E. Tr. p. 234).

but practical; it is not representation but virtual action. It is true that in the adult human consciousness perception and action appear to be entirely different, but examination shows that they differ only in degree, not in kind. This becomes apparent when we trace the progress of external perception through the ascending scale of living beings. In the lowest stages perception is mere contact issuing in necessary reaction from which consciousness is absent. There is here no differentiation —the organ of perception is also the organ of movement, and there is no variation in its response to stimuli. But higher up in the scale contact and reaction are no longer coincident, hence an element of indetermination enters— the action not being immediate may cease to be necessary. Thus "reaction" becomes "action" and perception arises. In proportion as reaction may be delayed, hence varied, consciousness becomes more intense, and with the choice of reactions there is perception, the extent of which is exactly proportioned to the amount of indetermination allowed so that we may say that "perception is master of space in the exact measure in which action is master of time." Perception, then, is possible action; it is in no sense representation.

We conclude then that there are in the material world—or system of "images"—living bodies which are "*centres of real action*" and that "around each of these centres are ranged images subordinated to its position and variable with it[1]," and, just because the images are subordinate to these centres of indetermination, it is obvious that "their mere presence is equivalent to the suppression of all those parts of the objects in which their

[1] *M. et M.* p. 18 (E. Tr. p. 21).

functions find no interest," while "the others [parts of objects] isolated, become 'perceptions' by their very isolation[1]." From the totality of images the living being isolates so much as interests his needs, neglecting what is useless, and from this isolation arises representation. Apart from a living being with its power of selective action, there is no perception, for the images "indifferent to each other because of the radical mechanism which binds them together...act and react mutually by all their elements," hence, "none of them, consequently, is perceived or perceives consciously[2]." But where the living body opposes their action there is perception, for "this diminution of their action is just the representation we have of them. Our representation of things would thus arise, in short, from the fact that they are thrown back and reflected against our freedom."

There is thus only a difference of degree, not of kind, between "being" and "being consciously perceived"; the perception of matter results from the elimination of all that does not concern the practical needs of the living body. In other words, perception is to matter as the part to the whole, the separation of the part being effected by the operation of bodily needs. On the other hand the difference between perception and feeling is one of kind, not merely of degree. Whereas perception is possible action, feeling is actual action; perception is without the body and is perceived there, feeling is within the body and is experienced there. Feeling is subjective, perception is objective and "in the pure state will make, then, veritably a part of things." As a matter of fact we never experience perception "in the pure state"; it

[1] *M. et M.* p. 24 (E. Tr. p. 28).   [2] *Ibid.* p. 25 (E. Tr. p. 29).

is always mingled with memory which gives to it a subjective character, the combination constituting "concrete perception"—the intersection of mind and matter.

. Into the difficulties raised by this theory of "pure perception," difficulties that are increased by the ambiguity of the word "image"—an ambiguity that is, however, essential to the theory in that it blurs over the distinction between the "act of perceiving" and "what is perceived," the recognition of which distinction would be fatal to the theory itself—it is not my purpose to enter. It is sufficient for the present inquiry if it has been made clear that from his examination of the nature of perception Bergson draws the conclusion that "the body, always turned towards action, has for its essential function to limit, with a view to action, the life of spirit[1]." This conclusion is further inforced in his view of intellect. From a study of its genesis in the course of the evolutionary movement, M. Bergson attempts to show that intellect is fashioned on materiality and "feels itself at home among inanimate objects, more especially among solids, where our action finds its fulcrum and our industry its tools[2]." It "triumphs in geometry" and, in a word, is adapted to "think matter." But we are concerned with matter only in so far as we can adapt it to our practical needs, i.e. act upon it. Hence "it is in the mould of action that intelligence has been formed" and "originally we think only in order to act[3]." It follows that the intellect deals adequately only with the discontinuous and motionless; life as a living reality escapes it, for the living must be regarded as inert before we can operate on it.

[1] *M. et M.* p. 197 (E. Tr. p. 233).   [2] *Ev. Cr.* p. i (E. Tr. p. ix).
[3] *Ibid.* p. 47 (E. Tr. p. 46).

The practical needs of action play, therefore, an important part in determining the general nature of our knowledge by reason of the "utilitarian character of our mental functions, which are essentially turned towards action[1]." The results of this influence may be briefly summed up as misrepresentation of the real due to (a) the division of matter into independent, isolated bodies which in their independence and isolation can be utilised by us; (b) the creation of homogeneous space and time as the diagrammatic schema of our possible action on matter, and this leads to an inversion of reality by which we make rest logically prior to movement; (c) the isolation of a "fact" as real, whereas it is an adaptation of the real in the interests of action; (d) the neglect of the past except in so far as it is practically useful, and the consequent narrowing down of consciousness to the present, i.e. to the state of our body; (e) the discontinuity of knowledge due to the requirements of discontinuous action, hence the erection of clear-cut "concepts" that deal only with the motionless and discontinuous, thus failing to give the movement of the living reality.

Similarly, practical needs and the requirements of social intercourse are the cause of the gradual submersion of the fundamental self, the free ego, by the superficial self that lends itself better to the exigencies of social life. It is because we are individuals in society that we neglect our deeper individuality in order to bring our conscious states to the level of discourse by means of which only is social life possible. In order that there may be a society of individuals an external world common to all of them and distinct from each must be formed. A confusion

[1] Introduction to Eng. Ed. of *Matter and Memory*, p. xvii.

where inner states interpenetrate is useless for social intercourse. But the fundamental self is just such a confused heterogeneity, hence, in the interests of society, a second, superficial self is formed.

The intellect, however, is above all the faculty of practical social life; its work is to procure the satisfaction of social and biological needs; it is bound to the service of practical activity. For this end it treats the living as if it were inert, it represents movement as a sum of immobilities, it spreads out the living self into a series of discontinuous, distinct conscious states, and finally, it subjects truth to the faculty of action.

By reason of its practical function intellect is powerless to give us knowledge of the real for it carries over into speculation the practical necessities of action thereby vitiating the results of our speculation by making it, also, relative to our action. M. Bergson holds that in so far as our apprehension is determined by the exigencies of practical life it is *mis*apprehension; the immediate necessities of action distort our apprehension of reality. Thus it appears to him that "the impotence of speculative reason, as Kant has demonstrated it, is perhaps at bottom only the impotence of an intellect enslaved to certain necessities of bodily life, and concerned with a matter which man has had to disorganise for the satisfaction of his wants. Our knowledge of things would thus no longer be relative to the fundamental structure of our mind, but only to its superficial and acquired habits, to the contingent form which it derives from our bodily functions and from our lower needs. The relativity of knowledge may not, then, be definitive. By unmaking that which these needs have made we may restore to intuition its original purity and thus recover contact with the real[1]."

This suggestion that intellect is rendered impotent for speculation by reason of its bondage to the necessities of bodily life is put to the proof in *Creative Evolution*. By a study of the genesis of intellect M. Bergson endeavours to show that it has been evolved solely for the purposes of action on matter, and that intellect and materiality are created by the same inversion of the same movement, and for this reason are progressively adapted one to the other.

We shall have occasion later to examine the bearing of this upon M. Bergson's theory of knowledge and to draw out the scepticism implicit in it. The conclusion that M. Bergson draws is that the philosopher must free himself from the tyranny of practical needs since, under their sway, he can only think matter, the inverse of the living reality, and must examine "the living without any reservation as to practical utility, by freeing himself from forms and habits that are strictly intellectual[2]." M. Bergson does not, then, conclude from the practical nature of intellect and its consequent inability to give us a theory of the real that no such knowledge is attainable. There is, he holds, another source of knowledge, for the line of evolution that has culminated in man is not the only one. Along other paths other forms of consciousness have developed each of which contains an essential element of the evolutionary process, and it may be, he suggests, that their amalgamation would result in "a consciousness coextensive with life" to which a complete, if fleeting, vision of life would be possible.

[1] *M. et M.* p. 203 (E. Tr. p. 241).
[2] *Ev. Cr.* p. 214 (E. Tr. p. 206).

In the course of its encounter with matter the "vital impulse" has developed two forms of consciousness, instinct and intellect, which correspond to the double form of the real. But while, as we have seen, intellect is held to be adapted to matter, instinct is peculiarly fitted to deal with life since "it only carries out further the work by which life organises matter, so that we cannot say... where organisation ends and where instinct begins." It would seem that here we have the faculty we require to penetrate the most intimate secrets of life. Unfortunately, however, instinct is not only dumb, it is unconscious and turned towards action, not towards knowledge. It cannot, therefore, disclose its secrets. But it is capable of developing into another faculty, that of intuition which is disinterested self-conscious instinct.

Since M. Bergson claims that by an effort of intuition it is possible for us to install ourselves within the current of life and thus gain knowledge of extra-intellectual reality, it is of the greatest importance to determine precisely what the nature of this intuition is, and to estimate its validity as a method of knowledge.

We may first briefly sum up the fundamental difference between instinct and intelligence. It may be expressed, on the side of action, as the difference between using—and even making—organic tools, and making and using inorganic, artificial tools. From the point of view of knowledge the distinction lies in the fact that instinct is the knowledge of a thing, intellect the knowledge of a relation ; the one deals with a matter, the other with a form. The first kind of knowledge is complete and full as far as it extends, but it is limited to a few things ; the second—intellectual knowledge—can extend over a wider

range just because it is an empty form into which anything may be fitted, but for this reason it is limited in
intension. They are thus complementary. Were they
fused, they would lead to complete and absolute knowledge, for intellect is fitted to seek, instinct to find.

2. M. BERGSON'S THEORY OF INTUITION AND THE
NOTION OF TRUTH IN THE "NEW PHILOSOPHY."

(1) M. Bergson has worked out his theory of intuition from two different standpoints—first, from the
point of view of philosophical method; secondly, from that
of the development of consciousness in the process of
evolution. The former statement occurs in an article—
entitled *Introduction à la Métaphysique*—published in
1903 in the *Revue de Métaphysique et de Morale*. This
article, although it contains M. Bergson's earliest account
of the nature of intuition and his most thorough examination of it as the method proper to philosophy, nevertheless
has not attracted nearly so much attention as the later
account in *L'Evolution Créatrice*.

But it seems to me to be of very great importance in
view of the fact that it contains no mention of instinct.
Whereas in *L'Evolution Créatrice* intuition is defined as
"instinct become disinterested, conscious of itself," while
intellect and instinct are diametrically opposed—for, " we
cannot too often repeat it, intellect and instinct are turned
in two opposite ways"—in this earlier account intuition is
described as "a kind of *intellectual sympathy*."

Before considering the significance of this divergence
in statement, we must refer briefly to the two accounts
given.

There are, M. Bergson says, in his *Introduction à la Métaphysique*, two different modes of knowing a thing. Either we can view it from outside by " turning round it," or we can "enter into it[1]." The knowledge gained by the first method depends upon the point of view of the observer, hence it remains external and relative; it is essentially the work of analysis which gives first one aspect, then another, but never the thing as a whole. The fact that what is thus attained remain "points of view," partial aspects seen from without, prevents us from attaining the essence of the thing we seek to know. If, on the other hand, the contention runs, we could for a moment "coincide with it" so as to see it from within, or rather to *be* it, then, and then only, should we know it absolutely.

The first way of knowing is that of the intellect analysing into concepts and expressing itself in symbols; the second is that of intuition, sympathetic insight whereby knower and known in some measure coincide. Only by thus becoming one with the thing can we know "what it properly is, what constitutes its essence."

Such knowledge, it will readily be admitted, is of the nature of *sympathy* in the fullest meaning of the word. M. Bergson describes it as[2] "this kind of *intellectual sympathy* by which one places oneself within an object in order to coincide with what is unique in it and consequently inexpressible," and he contrasts it with analysis which is "the operation which reduces the object to elements already known, that is, to elements common both

---

[1] " The first implies that we move round the object; the second that we enter into it," p. 1.

[2] *Int. Mét.* pp. 6—7 (E. Tr.).

to it and other objects....All analysis is thus a translation, a development into symbols, a representation taken from successive points of view." Such analysis is the method used by the positive sciences and admirably adapted for this practical purpose; metaphysics, however, must dispense with symbols which fail to give knowledge of the inner reality and must surrender itself to intuition or "intellectual sympathy."

When, however, we turn to the account of intuition in *L'Evolution Créatrice*, we find it sharply opposed to intellect, though sometimes described as the luminous fringe surrounding the nucleus of intellect, and itself partaking of the nature of instinct. The antagonism of intellect and instinct, however, is, as we have seen, brought out by Bergson with regard to their development along divergent lines of evolution, with regard to the kind of knowledge they are adapted to give—intellect dealing with *relations*, instinct with *things*—finally, with regard to their intrinsic nature—for, as M. Bergson sums it up— "There are things which intelligence alone is capable of seeking, but which, by itself, it will never find. These things instinct alone would find, but it will never seek them[1]."

Instinct will never seek them for it is blind and unconscious. It must be awakened into consciousness, it must be turned towards knowledge, it must become reflective and self-conscious; that is, it must become intuition. It can do this, M. Bergson maintains, for instinct is sympathy, a "feeling with" its object, and "if this sympathy could extend its object and also reflect upon itself, it would give us the key to vital operations,"

[1] *Ev. Cr.* p. 164 (E. Tr. p. 159).

for "it is to the very inwardness of life that *intuition* would lead us, I mean to say instinct become disinterested, self-conscious, capable of reflecting upon its object and of enlarging it indefinitely[1]."

From a comparison of these two accounts of intuition we see that it is essentially of the nature of sympathy, of "intuition" in its ordinary meaning of an insight that transcends logical formulation. Whether it is to be accounted a development of intellect—as M. Bergson would seem to have held in the earlier article; or, whether it is rather of the nature of instinct, as would appear from his later treatment, is largely a matter of words, for whatever may be the meaning that is usually attached to "instinct" it is not applicable to a reflective consciousness. The important point, however, is whether we may not consider that intuition is not *opposed* to intellect, but that it transcends it.

In a passage in the Introduction to *L'Evolution Créatrice* which refers to his theory of intuition, M. Bergson, speaking of the forms of consciousness, other than intellect, which have been developed in the evolutionary process, suggests that "in bringing these forms together, in making them fuse with intellect, should we not obtain then a consciousness as wide as life and capable, in turning around suddenly against the push of life which it feels behind, of obtaining a vision of life complete although undoubtedly fleeting[2]?" Even here, then, intuition appears to be the fusion of intellect and instinct, hence not in opposition to intellect. Nevertheless his whole point of view seems to demand that *intuition* and intellect, no less than *instinct*

---

[1] *Ev. Cr.* pp. 191—2 (E. Tr. p. 186).
[2] *Ibid.* p. v (E. Tr. p. xii).

and intellect, should be regarded as inverse and opposed, in spite of many passages in which he speaks as though intuition were the completion of intellectual knowledge, ultra-intellectual, indeed, but still *intellectual.* He is willing to go further and urges that " if there are thus two intuitions of different order (the second being obtained by a reversal of the direction of the first), and if it is toward the second that intellect naturally inclines, there is no essential difference between the intellect and this intuition itself[1]." The sharpness of the opposition between intuition and intellect which led to the relegation of the latter to an inferior plane is here overcome.

It is at this point that the close connection between theory of knowledge and theory of life—upon which M. Bergson insists—becomes important. Only by a study of the development of consciousness can we see that intellect and instinct are both one-sided developments from the vital impulse, specialised forms of consciousness which, alone, are impotent to fathom the nature of life but together will resolve the great problems of philosophy. Other forms of consciousness, however profound they may be, however near to reality, are yet, apart from intellect, powerless, and, it would seem, powerless in two ways: first, because only intellect has been able to free itself from external constraint, hence intellect alone is aware of a problem; secondly, only intellect can formulate the solution which however, if unaided, it is powerless to find. Consequently, we need both a theory of knowledge to criticise the work of intellect, and a theory of life, which, by showing us how the work of

[1] *Ev. Cr.* p. 389 (E. Tr. p. 381).

intellect has been accomplished, will enable us to go beyond it and complete it.

When, therefore, M. Bergson is claimed as an anti-intellectualist, it must be remembered that the "intellect" he condemns is a one-sided development, an intellect bound to the service of practical needs—in other words, pragmatic in structure. It is just because intellect is thus bound to practical utility that M. Bergson considers it disqualified for theoretical speculation and would replace it with intuition or intellectual sympathy the essential nature of which is disinterestedness on our part, absorption in the object for its own sake with no reference to utility.

How far this supra-intellectual intuition can be admitted and whether it is consistent with M. Bergson's view of the nature and function of intellect must be considered later. It will be convenient first, before passing on to M. Le Roy's notion of truth—the direct outcome of this theory of intuition—to consider whether the theory itself may not be regarded as a logical development from the philosophical position of Ravaisson and Maine de Biran.

(2) Ravaisson considers that the true philosophical method is not to proceed inductively from the phenomena of consciousness to their laws. To do so would be to make these internal phenomena external, hence to deprive them of their living reality and divorce them from the real self. The true method is that which distinguishes from the fact of a sensation or perception "that which completes it in making it ours, and which is no other than ourselves." In all of which we are conscious we must discern our own act. "When we enter," he says, "into ourselves, we find ourselves in the midst of a world

of sensations, of feelings, of imaginations, of ideas, of volitions, of memories,—a moving ocean without limits and without foundations, which nevertheless is wholly ours, which nevertheless is nothing other than ourselves." But he asks, " How ours ? how ourselves? Because at each moment and in each place of this multifold inward whirlpool, we form from its moving diversity wholes, whose bond is a unity that is no other than the very operation by which we form them[1]." Only by this synthetic operation and recoil on self can we reach the inner reality. Analysis neither of fact, as in Empiricism, nor of idea, as in Idealism, can attain it. The supreme reality is " the consciousness of this absolute formed by the inward activity, where reality and perfection coincide and coalesce into one." It is the constraining power of absolute perfection towards which our activity tends that gives us consciousness of ourselves as participating in this perfection which is " a universal God, who is absolute good and infinite love." This union with God is love which is the foundation and substance of the self and its end. We penetrate the ultimate reality because of our essential similarity with it, so that we can insert ourselves within it, and by an intuition of loving sympathy can grasp what lies beyond the comprehension of the intellect. Moreover, Ravaisson holds that God, the ultimate reality, lies beyond the comprehension of intellect just because the intellect is limited to " points of view " and cannot grasp from within " the absolute in which we participate." In this we may surely see a foreshadowing of M. Bergson's intuitionism whereby the knower must " enter into " the known.

[1] *La Phil. en France*, p. 243.

In his theory of the self Ravaisson developes an idea found in de Biran and later to be developed by M. Bergson in his doctrine of the profound ego from which his theory of intuition springs.

De Biran, as we have seen, found the essence of consciousness in will, or effort as experienced in voluntary activity. As Ravaisson points out, this involves a conscious being enduring in time and independent of space. It is this act of willing that is really "we ourselves" and which we reach, Ravaisson says, only when we divest ourselves of the results of habit. So, too, M. Bergson urges that we must pierce below the superficial ego that results from the habits and needs of social intercourse, to the profound ego that is alone real. The conclusion of both is that reality must be "immediately seized" or "intuited."

De Biran, however, in spite of this logical development from his theory of the self, shows no traces of a theory of supra-intellectual intuition. At first sight it might appear that this statement is contradicted by de Biran's recognition of two orders which he calls the "system of knowledge" and the "system of belief." But on closer examination it becomes evident that the "system of belief" that de Biran calls in to fill up the gaps in his theory of knowledge, does not play the part assigned to intuition by Ravaisson and M. Bergson.

De Biran had at first adopted so purely subjective a standpoint in taking the psychological fact of effort as the foundation of all knowledge, that he felt later the need of seeking a wider basis. This he found in the *belief* in objective realities.

We start, he said, with a belief in objective reality, and it is the task of philosophy to justify this belief and draw consequences from it. This task he attempted in a work, written in 1813 but not published till after his death, entitled *Rapports des Sciences Naturelles avec la Psychologie.* This work marks a new phase in his philosophy and the abandonment of pure empiricism. He had at first regarded the notions of soul and substance as the result of abstraction working on the primitive data of consciousness. But now he recognised in them suggestions of a superior and distinct-faculty of "belief." Thus beneath the system of "knowledge" given through the primitive fact of consciousness, there is a system of universal and necessary beliefs having for their object the absolute reality of objective existences which consciousness shows us only under their subjective and relative aspect. Hence "All that we know or can know has thus a necessary principle in what we do not know, but which we believe to exist in the absolute order, in the realm of existences[1]." For example, in the relative order of our knowledge, the original or primitive fact of consciousness, which comprises an effort willed and a resistance to it, implies a two-fold absolute existence, viz. (*a*) absolute activity of a substance or force which we admit without conceiving—i.e. the soul: (*b*) absolute resistance or inertia, i.e. body, and "we believe in these two existences, we are certain that they remain, that they endure when all effort, all resistance vanishes with the *self,* although we have no idea of this absolute outside of feeling or of present knowledge[2]."

In considering the question whether these two systems arise together, de Biran on the whole inclines to give the priority to knowledge over belief: "the self can exist and

<hr>

[1] *op. cit.* p. 166.   [2] *Ibid.* p. 166.

know itself without believing at first that it is bound to a substance," nevertheless, " if nothing absolute were given originally and necessarily, as object of belief, there would not be even relative knowledge, that is to say, that we should know nothing at all[1]."

In spite of the fact, however, that " our faculty of belief is bound by its nature to the *absolute*, that it is as a face of the human mind which finds itself naturally turned towards the absolute reality of things or of beings," yet it does not seem that de Biran considers this faculty as a sort of superior intuition by which we reach a reality otherwise inaccessible. Absolute reality is rather the unknowable. The new theory is, then, introduced rather to supply the notions of universality and necessity which were lacking in his earlier and purely empirical theory of knowledge. Universality is given by the necessity imposed on our minds of developing notions whose germs are given in primitive and immediate experience. For, de Biran argues, if men perceive somewhat in the same manner, is it not reasonable to suppose the existence of " original laws or of regulative and necessary principles, to which our understanding is subjected by its nature[2] " ?

(3) The theory of intuition is carried to an extreme by M. Le Roy by whom the notion of truth implicit in M. Bergson's metaphysic is explicitly developed. We have remarked that M. Bergson does not himself directly face the question as to the nature of truth, but in the philosophical writings of his disciples MM. Le Roy and Wilbois the conception of truth becomes the centre of discussion. In the course of examining this theory we shall consider the alleged relation between the pragmatic

[1] *Ibid.* p. 185.   [2] *Ibid.* p. 163.

theory of truth and the notion of truth in the "New Philosophy," and in this connection it will be convenient to consider the work of Professor Poincaré.

In the preface to *Studies in Humanism* (1906) Dr Schiller, reviewing the spread and development of Pragmatism on the Continent, declares that the new movement is most marked in France, "either in its properly pragmatic forms or in their equivalents and analogues." In support of this contention he cites the names of Professor Bergson, Professor Poincaré (with some reservations) and MM. Le Roy and Wilbois, the two latter of whom he describes as "ultra-pragmatic followers of Professor Bergson" (p. xi).

Now it is not difficult to show that in not one of these cases can the claim be substantiated. Although perhaps it is not easy to determine what precisely is included in the "equivalents and analogues" of "properly pragmatic forms," it is at least clear that the four French philosophers cited depart from the latter in just what constitutes the essence of Pragmatism, namely, its theory of Truth.

In the philosophy to which M. Le Roy has given the name of "La philosophie nouvelle" and which he sometimes describes as "un positivisme nouveau," elements appear which at first sight give it the appearance of Pragmatism, and isolated passages could be found which might have been written by Dr Schiller himself. Nevertheless, when we examine M. Le Roy's conception of truth we find that it is entirely different from the "James-Schiller" theory, and in opposition to it, being indeed a development from Bergson which is, however, ultra-Bergsonian, but, for that very reason, *not* " ultra-*pragmatic.*" The sole point that the two theories have in common is their anti-intellectualism, but even here the standpoint of each is different and is the result of opposite lines of reflection. This divergence, from the point of view of philosophical construction, is vital.

Dr Schiller founds Pragmatism on the assertion that "all mental life is purposive," and hence derives his conception of truth as a " value "—that is true which answers the purpose—admitting, however, that it is "*logical* value." Not only would M. Le Roy not admit "logical" value in truth, but the whole conception of purpose that plays so large a part in Dr Schiller's theory is absent from his. That science is founded upon purpose M. Le Roy would admit; it is his complaint that science aims at the satisfaction of our practical needs, and in so far as this purpose is fulfilled the real is "deformed" to suit our needs. Thus we attain utility but not truth. This need not trouble us since truth is not the aim of science, which seeks only the conquest of the world by manipulating it to suit our purposes. Science is thus "the attempt to construct a rational scheme of the aforesaid representation, a scheme through and by means of which we come by habit to perceive and to manipulate the elements of common experience[1]." Here "*the scheme will be called true if it fulfils its office*[2]. Scientific truth is thus, in ultimate analysis, only fidelity to the essential point of view which science itself defines; every proposition is true which agrees with it and contributes to bring it out more clearly. This truth is then entirely *relative*: to a certain intellectual attitude, to a certain orientation of thought,

---

[1] *R.M.M.* 1901, p. 560.

[2] Italics are M. Le Roy's unless otherwise stated.

to a certain purpose—very legitimate, doubtless, but not at all unique or preeminent."

This passage—and the whole discussion of which it forms a part—brings out exactly M. Le Roy's double point of view and the distinction he makes between the scientific point of view with the truth relative to it, and a more ultimate point of view not yet defined. It is from exclusive attention to the former that Dr Schiller is led to rank him as a pragmatist.

Science is, according to M. Le Roy, an elaboration of common sense knowledge, and he follows M. Bergson in regarding this as formed under the influence of practical necessities, that is, with direct reference to utility. Common sense knowledge springs from the " simple apprehension of things by their outside " and " the outside of things is the aspect which they turn to our action[1]." Science is but the systematisation and development of this: it makes no attempt to pierce to the bottom; its aim is solely power and its chief method is spatialisation, " space being only the general scheme of our power over nature." Since science seeks only practical manipulation of reality its sufficient criterion is " the satisfaction of our thought in view of its work[2]," and for its purposes all is true that " succeeds " for just so long as it *is* successful. But this, cannot be taken as absolute, for many of the notions of science " appear to a more profound reflection as symbolic representations spontaneously constructed, unconscious deformations of reality, translations of nature into the language of action which hold things only by the points in which our activity is concerned[3]." Thus "common

---

[1] *loc. cit.* p. 421.   [2] *Ibid.* p. 422.

[3] *Ibid.* p. 422.

knowledge is solely relative to Appearance, that is to the relation between the real and our power of acting[1]." Science is based on the need for organisation, *mise en ordre*; in other words—"Science is a device of mind for conquering the world." But it is not self-sufficient, for the mind seeks not only practical utility but a supreme unity which science—because of its dependence on our needs—is powerless to give.

Having submitted the knowledge derived from common sense and from science to a careful examination, M. Le Roy, then, draws the conclusion that "science and common sense are now behind us and still our intellectual satisfaction is not yet accomplished[2]." There is left philosophic intuition which will undo the work of science and practical life and put us into contact with the primitive reality uncontaminated by the influence of practical necessity.

There could not be any philosophical view more obviously anti-pragmatic. Science is organisation with a view to practical activity; philosophy is an intimate knowledge of the underlying reality—its purpose is to "awake in us the *sense of things*, to give us the *habit* and, as it were, the *instinct* of them, to lead us in some degree to *become* them and provide the means of living thus in their intimate familiarity[3]." Philosophy, then, must look in the exactly opposite direction, away from science and considerations of practical utility.

From this it would appear that if we were to stop short at science, we should be led to class M. Le Roy as a pragmatist, and from this point of view the claim could be well substantiated. He is even ultra-pragmatic in his

[1] *R.M.M.* 1899, p. 544.   [2] *Ibid.* p. 710.

[3] *Ibid.* p. 721.

assertions that scientific laws are " practical receipts," and hold only in so far, and for as long as, they are successful. On the other hand, he continually points out that just because they are practical adaptations, we cannot rest satisfied with them and regard them as final truths— " As practical receipts," he urges, " they are not *true* but *efficacious*; they concern less our knowledge than our *action*; they enable us to control the order of nature rather than to discover it[1]." And again, "the mind tends spontaneously to the *useful*, not to the true[2]."

If, then, the true is not to be identified with the useful, we must consider further what M. Le Roy takes the true to be. The pragmatic conception of truth having been rejected implicitly, for in formulating his conception of truth M. Le Roy never considers the equation of the true with the useful, he develops his own theory in opposition to the realistic notion .of truth. "The definition," he says, " which I condemn is this: truth consists in the conformity of thought with its object[3]." Here Being is opposed to Thought, but this, he holds, " renders all know-ledge impossible, all certainty illusory," for, in such case, " how shall we assure ourselves of an agreement between the representation and the object[4] ? " Hence he concludes " Thought is being itself, the efficient principle of all positing," so that " the object of affirmation coincides with the affirmation itself." Truth thus ceases to be a matter of the contemplation of an object ; it is *action*.

In thus defining Truth as "action " M. Le Roy seems once more to be taking up the pragmatist's position. He is aware that the ambiguity of the word may lead to

---

[1] *B.S.F.Ph.* 1901, p. 5.   [2] *R.M.M.* 1901, p. 141.
[3] *Ibid.* 1899, p. 560.   [4] *B.S.F.Ph.* 1904, p. 154.

misunderstanding, and from time to time he points out the different senses in which the word action may be used. There are three senses, which may be distinguished, viz.: (a) practical action, which engenders common sense knowledge; (b) discursive action which rules science; and finally (c) profound action which is the "action" in question in philosophy, and is defined as life, as love, as "lived-thought." It is of action in this sense that he speaks when he says—"I know that that which is best in man is his power of action[1]." Here he uses the same expression as before when calling attention to the distorting effects of our *"puissance d'agir"* on the reality thus manipulated. But the distinction is clear for he at once goes on to add "Now all profound and true action is love, devotion, gift of self: there is the real life." In a discussion at the French Society of Philosophy, the equivocation of the term "action" or "life" having been pointed out, M. Le Roy replied that the difficulty could be easily avoided—"It suffices to say *Thought-Action (Pensée-Action)*. The action to which I appeal, in fact, is not external, heterogeneous to thought; on the contrary, it implies thought; I said it just now: it is an action of thought; in short, it is thought in so far as active and productive[2]." He adopts, then, the term "thought-action" to differentiate it from practical or "industrial" action, and the distinction is essential to his philosophy, which, in a previous article (1901), he had described as a *"spiritualism"* in that it subordinated dead results to the living progress of thought, and as a *"positivism"* in the sense that "in his eyes the supreme criterion is action, doubtless not industrial action, nor even discursive action, but profound

[1] *R.M.M.* 1901, p. 425.　　　　[2] *B.S.F.Ph.* 1904, p. 168.

THE NATURE OF FRENCH VOLUNTARISTIC PHILOSOPHY 65

action, that is to say, the life of spirit[1]." Thus we may
call it indifferently "lived thought," "profound action"
or "thought-action," and in each case it may be defined
as "*the supra-logical mental activity* which directs invention[2]."

This profound action, the source of discursive thought,
though not itself discursive is manifested by imperfect
concepts each of which reveals it from afar. It is the
error of intellectualism to hasten towards clearness (*la
clarté*) whereas the New Philosophy turns the other way
and hastens towards action. For intellectualism clear
thought is the end, hence knowledge will be the work
of " discourse." In opposition to this the New Philosophy
affirms that to be fruitful thought must be lived, so that
consequently knowledge is not the attainment of clear
ideas but is rather "an effort and a movement for the
purpose of descending into the inner obscurity of things,
and of inserting oneself within the rhythm of their original
life[3]."

To bring out the divergence of these views M. Le Roy
takes the image of an " inner visual field." In the centre
is a luminous area of clear day, where "discourse" has
cleared up obscurities; around is the penumbra fading
into darkness which we call action and life (p. 299). All
agree, M. Le Roy says, that we must increase the luminous
area, but the question is how ? Rationalism—or intellectualism—tries to do this by projecting the light it
already has, i.e. by way of concepts ; hence it makes *light*
supreme, whereas it should be *movement*. The New
Philosophy, then, turns in the other direction and aims at
action *because* "what is clear is no longer interesting,

[1] *loc. cit.* p. 147. [2] *Ibid.* p. 152. [3] *Ibid.* p. 297.

S. P.   5

since that is the purpose to which every work is directed, or at least it offers no more than an interest relative to the practical point of view of discourse[1]."

Is not M. Le Roy inconsistent here? Formerly he seemed to seek the obscure for its own sake, now he says that all agree that the luminous area must be increased, and that here the penumbra plays the essential *rôle* "somewhat in the manner of a final cause," since only the obscure needs to be made clear. All progress in philosophy, he says, has been gained by a victory over the obscure and contradictory by making it intelligible. The end would thus seem to be clearness, yet the obscure ceases to be interesting as soon as it becomes clear! What is the end the clearness is supposed to serve?

Changing the metaphor M. Le Roy compares the clear ideas to the *rungs* of a ladder, and says that to take them as the essential is to mistake the rungs for the energy of the man who mounts. Discursive thought is an instrument of knowledge, just as the steps are a means for climbing the ladder. It now appears that the *energy* is the end, and that nothing corresponds to the top. Presumably, when the top is reached interest will cease, just as before it was found that interest ceased when the obscurity was enlightened. The difficulty is not that energy or activity is taken as the end, but that it is apparently directed towards a purpose that defeats itself —unless indeed its sufficiency lies in the fact that it acts as a spur to activity, directed to no other end than its own continuance. There would then seem to be no top: the ladder would be endless and the climber need not fear that interest will cease, since he will never reach the

[1] *Ibid.* p. 304.

top. That this is M. Le Roy's view would appear from a passage in which he points out that " all true progress in philosophy consists in enlarging the concepts of the intellect and in causing light to be thrown upon what had, till then, seemed obscure," and goes on to add " in other words, to know is not so much to project an *a priori* light on things as to produce the light itself which our vision will use....Then a fact of capital importance appears : *discursive thought is subordinated to action and the clear to the obscure*[1]."

Thus, finally, we are led to sum up M. Le Roy's conception of Truth as life, movement itself. "Truth," he says, " is *life*, thus *movement*; *growth* rather than *limit*; the characteristic of certain *processes* rather than of certain *results*[2]." Hence there is nothing permanent in truth; it is continuous change, relative to the moment, the transitory expression of a fleeting movement. Nor does he mean by the changingness of truth that it is incomplete and may be developed by a *fuller* view, hence rendered complete. Truth is never "*faite*"; it is the life of mind, the series of its experiences; it is "a progressive verification rather than a completed truth[3]."

If truth is life, can there be any error ? It would seem that all is true. Nevertheless the existence of error cannot be denied, hence a criterion of truth must be sought. This is found in life itself—" in every case life alone conditions, clarifies and verifies. At bottom the sole criterion is life[4]." The only way to determine what is true is to *live* it. M. Le Roy goes further. Having pointed out that mistake will arise unless "life" be

[1] *Ibid.* p. 303. [2] *Dogme et Critique*, p. 355.
[3] *Ibid.* p. 356. [4] *R.M.M.* 1901, p. 317.

rightly conceived, i.e. unless it be "acted" and not transformed into the *concept* of action,—he concludes that "if one has not lived beforehand the doctrine I have just summed up, *one ought not* to understand it[1]." This obviously removes the criterion altogether. Life is at once Truth and the criterion of Truth.

I think, however, that when we remember the contention of the New Philosophy that to *know* an object one must *be* it, that truth is intuitively seized, it does not seem necessary to provide a criterion at all, for error would seem impossible. Necessary or not, however, the criterion cannot be found; to take "life" for it is obviously absurd.

M. Le Roy, it seems to me, perceives this, and leaving out of consideration the question of a criterion, he asserts that error is always the result of practical needs and social intercourse, but if we pierce below them we reach the flow of life which is truth, where no question of error can arise. Thus, he says, " error springs always from limitations due to discursive thought or to practices occasioned by action. Action taken in itself, in its pure state, could not be doubted. It grasps being adequately since it posits it and constitutes it. And I add that there is no incoherence to be feared so long as action remains fully and purely itself, for it is then *duration*, that is to say successive development, living continuity[2]."

Such "Truth" does not *need* a criterion, and it would seem that M. Le Roy only tries to find one when he looks away from his conception of "Truth" to the errors that arise in everyday life. This, of course, Dr Schiller would admit, but it only goes to prove the contention that the origin of their views is different.

To sum up M. Le Roy's relation to Pragmatism. He asserts that scientific facts are "conventions," that formulas and laws are " receipts for practical action," and hold only in so far as they are useful for that purpose, i.e. for so long as they " work"; in religion he asserts the practical nature of dogmas and holds that their value is, from the intellectual point of view, purely negative, i.e. they only condemn errors the consequence of which would be harmful —their purpose is not to augment our knowledge but to assign a direction to spiritual life.

Were he a pragmatist, M. Le Roy would stop here, and, having found something that is " useful," he would call it " true," since for the pragmatist " truth " *means* relevance and adequacy for practical needs. But M. Le Roy denies this, and expressly declares that the purpose of science being to render nature "agissable " for us, its value lies in its efficacy, but that it is not true. It is just because he thus holds that science has no claim to ultimate truth that he adopts a "mysticism," and concludes that " on l'échappe au scepticisme dans la mesure où l'on abandonne l'intellectualisme[1]." His search is for something that is not *merely* useful but also *true*. If he fails to find it, that is no reason for classing him as a prag-matist.

In common with M. Le Roy—with whom he is in close agreement—M. Wilbois describes his philosophy as " a new positivism," and he explicitly connects it with " Comtean positivism," at the same time claiming that it is " new " because based on a truer conception of fact that

[1] *R.M.M.* 1899, p. 327.

leaves room for human freedom. Whereas Comte accepted facts as "given," the "New Positivists" recognise them as arbitrary creations, fabrications of the mind.

M. Wilbois' philosophical position is stated in a series of articles entitled *L'esprit positif*[1]. In an article on *La méthode des sciences physiques*[2], M. Wilbois deals with the conception of "fact" with especial reference to physics, pointing out at the same time, however, that his remarks apply to all sciences. A "fact," he holds, is an arbitrary symbol, whether it be a "fact" as recognised by common sense, or a "physical fact." The only difference between the two classes of "fact" is that the physical is *more* arbitrary, *more* symbolical, hence farther from the underlying reality. A physical fact is a symbolised perception. These symbols are freely chosen by the scientist, his object being to reduce the "real" to a manageable form, hence to obtain "facts" that he can group into "laws." It follows that scientific laws are symbolic and arbitrary, so that "progress in science consists in approaching towards artificiality[3]," i.e. in going farther and farther from the real. There is no necessity in science except the necessity we put there to further our own purpose. The necessity itself of scientific laws results from our freedom, and is an argument in favour of it. It is the recognition of this, resulting from the new conception of fact as our invention, that constitutes, M. Wilbois considers, the advance of the "new" positivism on the "old."

Since "the stability of certain physical laws does not then depend upon the fixity of our mind or of our habits,

[1] Published in the *Revue de Métaphysique et de Morale*, 1901—1902.
[2] *R.M.M.* 1899, 1900.
[3] *Ibid.* 1901, p. 181.

these laws are immutable only so far as they are artificial[1]," it follows that science can give us no knowledge of the "real," that is, M. Wilbois adds, "the real in the Bergsonian sense[2]"; its work is "wholly practical."

Further, since all scientific theories are only symbolic, and laws are only arbitrary decrees of the scientist, it follows that we have no means of determining which of several contradictory theories—each of which explains the facts equally well—is, in any given case, the right one, or—rather—*all* are right in so far as they fit the facts, and *none* is "*true.*" The theory chosen will be the one that best suits the scientist's "character," hence we see characteristic differences in theories adopted, e.g. by the French and those adopted by the English, each being the reflection of the national character. A theory is only a language and a point of view arbitrarily chosen; thus "la théorie, c'est l'homme même, et c'est dans ce sens qu'on peut dire que chaque savant a son style[3]."

But although the theory is not true or false in the absolute sense, nevertheless it is symbolic, and experience fixes little by little all the properties of the symbol. Experience itself, then, imposes a limit on our arbitrary choice of symbols; it is not a perfect fluid that resists equal pressures equally in all directions, but rather a crystal that yields to pressure in one direction more easily than in another[4]. We cannot, therefore, verify any law, chosen haphazard, by multiplying its conditions to make it fit, for there are some to which matter was predisposed.

M. Wilbois, accordingly, in discussing Euclidean and

---

[1] *R.M.M.* 1900, p. 306.   [2] *Ibid.* p. 306 n.
[3] *Ibid.* 1899, p. 614.   [4] See *loc. cit.* p. 636.

non-Euclidean conceptions of space, recognises a distinction between them from this point of view. " Le postulatum d'Euclide," he says, "n'est pas un axiome de logique, comme le principe d'identité, ni un postulat arbitraire, comme le postulat de Lowatchewski; il contient une part d'expérience, aucune expérience ne le *prouve*, mais l'expérience journalière le *suggère*; il tient de notre esprit et des choses[1]."

In thus making a distinction between the *arbitrary* postulate of Lowatchewski, and the Euclidean postulate as being " *suggested* by experience," it seems to me that M. Wilbois would be forced to admit that the latter is more " convenient " in the sense of being nearer to the reality it symbolises. If all postulates as to the nature of space were equally arbitrary, then it might be said we *choose* one which happens to suit our point of view; but if one is to be recognised as peculiarly suitable to " our " habits, it would seem to correspond to something in the nature of reality which the other postulates lack. The pragmatist of course would be willing to accept this, and would say just because it is suited to our needs the Euclidean postulate is "true," but M. Wilbois—in common, as we shall see, with M. Poincaré—is careful to point out that just because a postulate is thus selected in accordance with our needs it cannot be " true " if by that we mean anything else than more or less useful. They are anxious to attain a truth that shall be independent of our needs, and if anything be shown to be relative to these it is, for that very reason, to be rejected as *not* ultimately true.

It appears, then, that having adopted a pragmatic

[1] *R.M.M.* 1899, p. 601. Italics are M. Wilbois'.

standpoint in science, M. Wilbois feels the need of going beyond it to obtain truth. His conclusion is that "il est vrai encore que l'examen des tendances générales de la physique nous montre une des façons dont l'homme cherche à dominer choses; la science apporte ainsi sa contribution à la psychologie ; mais ce fait, si important pour notre orgueil, est bien petit pour notre savoir. Et voilà tout le réel que la science apprend à connaître...la science, en effet, poursuivant une œuvre pratique dans un domaine fermé, ce n'est qu'à l'aide de malentendus et par surprise qu'on peut la heurter à la métaphysique[1]." Metaphysics and science are then to be severed.

MM. Wilbois and Le Roy, in common with M. Bergson, reject, then, the utilitarian standpoint in metaphysics. From the point of view of action we obtain a representation of the universe as the result of a utilitarian coordination of the elements of experience. Pure knowledge of the real, however, cannot be attained unless we turn our backs on practical requirements and abstract from the conditions of utility. So far from agreeing with the pragmatist in the identification of the true and the useful, the exponents of the New Philosophy go to the other extreme and utterly divorce the useful from the true. Thus M. Bergson says, "Just because this parcelling of the real has been effected in view of the exigencies of practical life, it has not followed the internal lines of the structure of things[2]"—a statement that is assuredly anti-pragmatic, however little justifiable in its conclusion !

No better case can be made out for the claim to include Prof. Poincaré among the adherents of Pragmatism. In naming the progenitors of the New Philosophy

[1] *R.M.M.* 1900, p. 322.   [2] *M. et M.* p. 202 (E. Tr. p. 240).

M. Le Roy[1] classes Prof. Poincaré, with MM. Boutroux and Milhaud, in the epistemological and critical current from which it is partially derived, and supports his own position in scientific procedure by frequent references to him. While to some extent Prof. Poincaré is willing to accept this position, yet he definitely rejects both the extreme "nominalism" of M. Le Roy and the anti-intellectualism of the New Philosophy.

In his work *La Science et l'Hypothèse*, Prof. Poincaré treats of the *rôle* of hypothesis in science, and points out the methodological nature of its axioms. By an examination of the possibility of non-Euclidean geometries, he attempts to show that geometrical space is a construction of the intellect under the influence of practical needs; its certainty, therefore, is the hypothetical certainty of deduction from given premisses. *Which* assumption—or axiom —we shall set out from is determined entirely by considerations of convenience. There is no geometrical space given us by experience or imposed on us *a priori*; we attain it by a fusion of visual, tactile and motor "spaces" in which differences are neglected in such manner as to give us the best perceptions of external objects. To ask further whether Euclidean space—or some other space—is true is to ask an absurdity, for "Une géométrie ne peut pas être plus vraie qu'une autre; elle peut seulement être *plus commode*[2]." Constituted as we are, Euclidean geometry is the most convenient, since it is simplest and fits in best with our activities. But it is not "true."

In his *La Valeur de la Science* Prof. Poincaré pursues further his consideration of the nature of space and its

---

[1] *R.M.M.* 1901, p. 293. [2] *op. cit.* p. 266.

dimensions, and once more concludes "l'expérience ne nous prouve pas que l'espace a trois dimensions; elle nous prouve qu'il est commode de lui en attribuer trois, parce que c'est ainsi que le nombre des coups de pouce est réduit au minimum[1]."

It is the third part of this book in which Prof. Poincaré expounds his views of the nature of law and the objective value of science, that is of chief interest for our present purpose. He begins by denouncing "nominalism" and "anti-intellectualism" as represented by M. Le Roy under the influence of Bergson.

Nominalism—the view that science is a work of arbitrary convention, that facts and laws alike are the "work" of the scientist and serve merely as "rules of action"— holds, Prof. Poincaré says, only to a very limited degree. It cannot be maintained that science gives us only rules for action if it meant thereby that the rules are selected *arbitrarily* as the rules of a game. The *facts* determine the rules, and the rules give knowledge of the facts. In so far as a "rule of science" is useful for action, it predicts facts, and thus has value as a means of knowledge. This criticism holds, even if we admit that action is the end of science. Prof. Poincaré, however, maintains that the end is knowledge in which action is a means. "À mes yeux, au contraire, c'est la connaissance qui est le but, et l'action qui est le moyen[2]."

The logical outcome of nominalism, Prof. Poincaré perceives to be scepticism. M. Le Roy saves himself, he says, only by appealing to the heart. Such anti-intellectualism is itself inadmissible and but a half-way house to scepticism.

[1] *op. cit.* p. 125.   [2] *Ibid.* p. 220.

Moreover—and here we have Prof. Poincaré's attitude clearly expressed—science is by its very nature intellectualistic—"by definition, so to say, it will be intellectualistic or it will not be[1]." To assert that "words" deform, that intellect distorts the things it deals with, is to cut off all possibility of science in every sense of the term. While it is true, on the one hand, that "there are in man other forces than his intellect," on the other, these "forces" are blind, *unknown* until dealt with by the intellect. Man must use his intellect *to see himself act*. A truly anti-intellectualist philosophy is thus impossible.

Prof. Poincaré thus concludes that science is possible and that it has objective value. Two questions arise: (*a*) With what does science deal? i.e. of what does it give us knowledge? (*b*) What is objectivity? The answer to the second question determines the answer to the first. Objectivity, Prof. Poincaré replies, is that which is common to several, it may be to all, thinking minds, hence *transmissible* from one to another. What then is transmissible? We see at once that sensation in so far as quality is *not* transmissible, but only the relations between sensations—the cementing bond which constitutes a group of sensations into an "object." ("It is this bond, and this bond alone in them which is an object, and this bond is a relation," p. 266.) Hence "the true relations between these real objects are the only reality that we can obtain[2]."

Science is thus a system of relations, and it does give us the *true* relations of things. It is, therefore, *true*, and it is *objective* for only these relations can be objective, and only what is objective can be known. Further it is real,

[1] *Ibid.* p. 217.   [2] *La Sc. et l'Hyp.* p. 190.

i.e. it is objective reality. To ask whether this reality can exist apart from minds that know it is meaningless, for "objectivity" *means* "what is common to several thinking beings, and is capable of being common to all[1]."

To sum up. In claiming Prof. Poincaré as an adherent of Pragmatism, Dr Schiller admits that he "imposes some slight limitations on the pragmatic treatment of knowledge, on the ground that knowledge may be conceived as an end to which action is a means," and bases the claim on the fact that Prof. Poincaré expounds the "pragmatic nature of the scientific procedures and assumptions[2]." But the reservation thus made is fatal.

While it is true that Prof. Poincaré's admission of the methodological nature of mathematics, his conception of the "principles" of science as convenient assumptions, and of science itself as a system of relations which are selected on the score of utility, seem to lead in the direction of Pragmatism, yet—on the other hand—not only is his view of the relation between knowledge and action distinctly *anti*-pragmatic, but, further, he admits utility—where he does admit it—*instead of* truth. He does not say that it is true because it is useful. Until, then, his views as to the nature of truth are more fully expounded it is not possible to rank Prof. Poincaré as a pragmatist. Indeed he has in a marked degree the intellectualist temper upon which Dr Schiller pours such scorn. "The scientist," Prof. Poincaré says, "does not study nature because it is useful; he studies it because he finds pleasure in it, and he finds pleasure in it because it is beautiful," and this beauty is an intellectual beauty that "a pure intelligence can seize," and, he concludes, "intellectual beauty suffices

1 *La Valeur de la Sc.* p. 9.   2 *loc. cit.*

for itself and it is for it, more perhaps than for the future welfare of humanity that the scientist condemns himself to long and laborious work[1]." It appears, then, that the anti-pragmatic elements in Prof. Poincaré's philosophy are too strong ever to allow it consistently to develope in such a way as to bring him into line with Pragmatism.

A comparison of the "New Positivism" of MM. Le Roy and Wilbois with the "old," or Comtean, positivism will, I think, show that the differences are more important than the resemblances and will further bring out the relation to pragmatism.

The characteristics of the Positive Philosophy may be found, Comte says[2], in the meaning of "positive" as real (i.e. as opposed to chimerical), useful, certain, precise and "positive" (i.e. opposed to "negative"), and, to these may be added, as a further characteristic of Positivism, its conversion of absolute into relative conceptions, relative, that is, to human society as the centre, or focus, of philosophy, and relative in that, our study of phenomena being "always relative to our organism and our situation," the search for ultimate causes is abandoned. "To conceive all our speculations as products of our intelligence, destined to satisfy our diverse essential needs" is, Comte says, "the attitude of a truly positive philosophy," and his position is summed up in the motto "Voir pour prévoir."

This is in radical opposition to MM. Wilbois and Le Roy who adopt, in its fullest extent, M. Bergson's theory of intuition as an attempt to *voir pour voir*. Thus M. Le Roy says, " I would agree willingly with M. Bergson that one can and one must accustom oneself to think being

---

[1] *Science et Méthode*, p. 15.

[2] *Discours sur l'Esprit Positif*, Pt. I. Sect. vii.

directly, for itself and not on our own behalf; that one can and one must strive to see for the sake of seeing, and no longer to see for the sake of action and utility. This effort of disinterestedness is the essential work of philosophy[1]."

So, too, M. Wilbois lays stress on the need of the Bergsonian regression, if we are to come into contact with reality. Comte, on the other hand, abandons the search for the real nature of things, for "causes" as distinct from laws which bind phenomena together, and denounces the "sterile erudition" which deals with science from any other point of view than that of rational prevision. "Thus," he says, "the true positive spirit consists chiefly in *seeing for the sake of foreseeing*, in studying what is for the purpose of concluding what will be[2]."

In thus renouncing all questions prompted by a sterile curiosity—hence admitting the existence of "useless" knowledge; and in linking the useful with the real and the humanly knowable, Comte seems in agreement with the modern pragmatist. But he makes no attempt to consider epistemological questions arising out of his view of the sciences; he does not ask what is the ultimate foundation of this positive knowledge, by what test we can determine its validity. He is content to say that truth is relative, that "our doctrines never represent the external world with extreme exactness." His position is thus rather agnostic than pragmatic, although, no doubt, dicta could be drawn from his works to support pragmatic pretensions. There is much in the attitude of old and new positivist alike that appears pragmatic until we examine the meaning they respectively attribute to truth. The Comtean positivist

[1] *B.S.F.Ph.* 1908, p. 274. [2] *Discours*, Pt. I. Sect. iii.

says: "If there be a real, absolute truth, we cannot know it, and we don't want it." The pragmatist says: "There *is* truth, or rather, "truths," and we not only know them, but we *make* them." The "new positivist" agrees that there is absolute truth but denies that it is to be found by means of the utilitarian procedure of the sciences; truth must be sought, he contends, by diving into the underlying flux, and to do this, the consideration of what is useful and practical must be left behind.

We conclude, then, that the New Philosophy is not Pragmatism. In calling itself a "new positivism" it appears to neglect a radical difference that separates it from Comtean positivism, for, it claims above all to be a "metaphysic" that reaches the real by means of an intuitive method that Comte would have utterly repudiated.

A closer parallel exists between the New Philosophy and Aristotle's doctrine of νοῦς ποιητικός. The conception of "living the real," which is fundamental to the New Philosophy, bears a striking resemblance to Aristotle's conception of θεωρία. To "live the real" is the supreme end-in-itself, and in it there is no opposition between knower and known but a union that is deeper than knowledge and in which the knower may be said to "know" his object only because he *is* it.

Such a view would seem to come direct from Aristotle, however different may be its formulation from a passage such as the following: "And thought thinks itself because it shares the nature of the object of thought; for it becomes an object of thought in coming into contact with and thinking its objects, so that thought and object of thought are the same[1]."

[1] *Metaphysica*, XII. vii.

It is true that with Aristotle the stress lies on "thought" and he has been regarded as the source of "intellectualism," nevertheless there is a marked affinity between his doctrine of contemplative activity and the latest modern theory of "profound action." Both, too, in the end, fall back on the conception of "life" to express its essential meaning. Thus Aristotle says—"for the actuality of thought is life, and God is that actuality; and God's essential actuality is life most good and eternal[1]." So, too, M. Le Roy uses "life," "lived-thought," "lived-action" and "thought-action" as synonymous for "profound action" or "living the real" which is truth.

M. Bergson also seems to find the highest life in "seeing for the sake of seeing[2]," and holds only that intelligence, i.e. discursive reason, is inadequate to the task. He, too, seeks an activity in which knower and known would be one. There must be no reference to practical activity. For M. Bergson and his disciples, no less than for Aristotle, contemplative activity appears as incomparably superior to practical activity, and perhaps each might conclude with the words: "This contemplation would seem also to be the only activity which is loved for its own sake, for it has no result beyond the act of contemplation, whereas from the active energies we gain something more or less beyond the performance of the action itself[3]."

The conception of θεωρία and "voir pour voir" cannot, however, by any means be brought into harmony with Pragmatism.

We are forced, then, to reject Dr Schiller's claim to rank the "New Philosophy" among the "equivalents and

[1] *Metaphysica*, XII. vii.   [2] See *Ev. Cr.* p. 323.
[3] *Ethics*, x. vii.

analogues " of Pragmatism. There is a marked tendency among Pragmatists to claim all those who emphasise the activity of mind as allies on every point *essential* to Pragmatism and to dub all their opponents, without discrimination, as " Intellectualists." Because Bergson regards intellect as subservient to the activity of life, as " an annex of the faculty of action," he is therefore claimed as a pragmatist. But we have seen that this cannot be maintained. To urge that consciousness has always a practical reference is not to say that only the practical is true. Bergson, indeed, urges that just because our ordinary knowledge is practical, it is *not true*. He lays stress on the practical nature of intellect only to discredit it for the service of truth ; he points out the influence of our practical needs upon speculation only to urge the importance of emancipation from them in the theoretical domain. He carries the antinomy of knowledge and action to an extreme, endeavouring thereby to free the former from the exigencies of the latter. This, then, is not Pragmatism.

So, too, M. Le Roy is pressed into the service of Pragmatism, but in spite of the many striking points of agreement between his view of the nature of science and that of the pragmatist there is a fundamental distinction which shows that the title is quite ineptly applied. He is assiduous in pointing out that scientific facts are " conventions " and hold only in so far as they are useful or " work "; in religion he asserts the practical nature of dogmas and denies them any positive value from the intellectual point of view. But he does not stop here, as, were he correctly speaking a pragmatist, he would. Under the influence of Bergson he goes on to urge that truth cannot be known but only lived, and that to " live it " practical needs must be transcended; they only *falsify* the real.

For the pragmatist, however, what satisfies practical needs *is* " true," for "truth" *means* relevance and adequacy for practical needs. When he has found something that is " useful," the pragmatist calls it " true " and denies that, in that direction, there can be any further truth. M. Le Roy, on the other hand, having found "facts" and "laws" that are " *convenient* " calls them " profitable fictions " or " working hypotheses," and even, in some moments of unguarded speech, " *scientific* truths." But he at no time regards such scientific truths as ultimate, but looks beyond to a " Truth " that is not *merely* useful but also *true*, and which can be attained, not by following the direction of practical needs, but by means of life which is essentially the activity of love, for, to know the truth is to " live the real."

3. THE " PHILOSOPHIE DE L'ACTION ": MM. BLONDEL AND LABERTHONNIÈRE.

In the course of this study the word " Pragmatism " has been used to denote the theory of truth that is now inseparably bound up with the names of William James and Dr F. C. S. Schiller. The word itself has, however, undergone various vicissitudes, and, by a curious coincidence, was coined anew in France before it had appeared in print in America.

As we have pointed out, the American originator of the word, Mr C. S. Peirce, used it to denote a method for " making our ideas clear " by developing the consequences they are fitted to produce. In the articles[1] expounding

---

[1] In the *Popular Science Monthly*, 1877—78.

this method the word "pragmatism" was not used, and the doctrine itself seems to have attracted no notice until, twenty years later, Prof. James brought it forward with special application to religion. In an interesting paragraph in an article published in the *Hibbert Journal* (Oct. 1908) Mr Peirce refers to the gradual change in the meaning of the term which he had invented in 1871, and used frequently in conversation, but only once in print (in Baldwin's Dictionary). But Prof. James having "transmogrified it into a doctrine of philosophy" which, in its "more prominent parts," Mr Peirce did not approve, he disowned "pragmatism" and renamed his own doctrine "pragmaticism" in 1905[1].

Meanwhile, in France M. Blondel had, in 1888, coined the word "*pragmatisme*" to denote a philosophy of action that, not only was conceived independently and in entire ignorance of Peirce's doctrine, but has no point of contact with it, and is directly opposed to its development by James and Schiller.

The French Society of Philosophy when engaged in 1902, in drawing up a philosophical vocabulary, discussed the advisability of framing a new term to denote the use of "action" in metaphysical theories such as that expressed by M. Blondel in his work *L'Action*. M. Blondel himself proposed the words "*pragmatique*" and "*pragmatisme*." The Society, however, refused to admit the term, on the ground that to do so would be to consecrate a doctrine which they did not accept! The word was, therefore, not included. In this discussion no reference was made to Anglo-American pragmatism, and the Society appeared to be in ignorance of the previous use of the term. Six

[1] The *Monist*.

years later, however, M. Parodi proposed for discussion by the Society, " *La Signification du Pragmatisme*," owing to the fact that "pragmatism seems to hold a more and more important place in Anglo-Saxon speculation[1]." The doctrines of James, Schiller and Dewey were examined and their connection with the "philosophy of action " of M. Blondel and M. Laberthonnière was regarded as obvious In a letter written to the Society, and printed in the Appendix to the *Bulletin*, M. Blondel protested strongly against such an affiliation, pointing out that essential differences exist between the two doctrines, and, in consequence, to mark this divergence, he was led, like Peirce, to abandon his original term[2], and substituted for it "*philosophie de l'action.*"

It will be advisable, then, to state briefly the main features of M. Blondel's philosophy, to examine his reasons for repudiating Pragmatism, and finally to consider whether the philosophies are allied and wherein they differ.

The aim of M. Blondel's philosophy is to discover what is ultimately involved in the fact of " action " itself, that is, of action regarded, not as *particular* actions, fragmentary and discontinuous, but rather "the single action which underlies and is expressed in the particular actions[3]." Action thus understood is the centre of man's life, and is preeminently the object of philosophy which must deal

---

[1] *B.S.F.Ph.* 1908, p. 249.

[2] "It is true," M. Blondel says, "that, from 1888, without having come across it anywhere, I have made use of the term pragmatism, firmly believing that I had coined it....Since the term 'pragmatism' has now acquired historically quite a different meaning, it has become necessary to free it completely from a verbal similarity which only provokes misunderstanding." (*B.S.F.Ph.* 1908, pp. 293—4 n.)

[3] *B.S.F.Ph.* 1902, p. 190.

with life, and not with thought alone, a partial abstract of action. Moreover, we do not "act for the sake of acting," but we act for the sake of what goes beyond the particular act, for action is not wholly self contained. There is in it an element of "passion," or "suffering," due to resistance encountered, since all action arouses hostility and is evoked by opposition. Action thus presupposes a reality beyond[1]. Moral action implies resistance and consciousness of power to overcome resistance, hence it involves a reality that transcends the world in which we act.

So, too, in the realm of science antinomies are solved if we remember that science cannot be limited to what it knows because it is already more than it knows. Science requires the postulate of action to unite it into a whole, by an internal principle of action "which eludes positive knowledge at the moment at which it makes it possible, and which, in a word that needs to be better defined, is a *subjectivity*[2]." Action *can* thus constitute a bond because external phenomena are of no other stuff (*étoffe*) than internal, hence "the subject is scientifically bound to the object, and contains it, and transcends it[3]." But since action is by its very nature unique, we cannot reduce it to fact, and deal with it as the positive sciences deal with their data. It is not the *result* of synthesis, but the living synthesis itself. It cannot, therefore, be studied, for "one penetrates the living reality only in placing oneself at the dynamic point of view of the will[4]."

M. Blondel traces in great detail the series of acts

---

[1] " It is not the will that causes what is; far from that, in so far as it wills it implies something which it does not make ; it wills to be what it is not yet." (*L'Action*, p. 43 n.)

[2] *L'Action*, p. 87.   [3] *Ibid.* p. 97.   [4] *Ibid.* p. 100.

from the individual action through social action to "superstitious" action, in which man tries to complete his action and suffice to himself. But, because in human action there is never an equality between the power and the wish, man is compelled to pass beyond to complete his activity in an act of absolute faith in the Ultimate Reality which is God. By means of action is thus derived the idea of a Being immanent in man, because his action is his own will, and yet transcendent, because the goal of his action is not given in the objective world of understanding. The aim of M. Blondel's philosophy is thus distinctly religious; his endeavour is to show that even the simplest acts of everyday life must lead us on to a final act of religious faith, and that, by means of action, may be solved the problem of reconciling the immanence of God with His transcendence.

M. Blondel repeatedly protests against the description of this philosophy of action as *alogical*. He does not desire to oppose action to knowledge, nor to *prefer* the former. Rather, he says, " the progress of action causes the progress of thought, as the progress of thought conditions and determines the progress of action[1]." His purpose in studying action is " to make more and more profoundly *intelligible* what is not immediately and specifically *intellectual*[2]."

Such a philosophy is, he considers, at the antipodes of Anglo-American pragmatism, both as to method and aim. He accuses pragmatism of failure in that it makes of action an extrinsic criterion of truth, thereby involving ambiguity in the interpretation of the criterion. It thus fails to be a true philosophy of *action* and remains a *theory*

[1] *B.S.F.Ph.* 1902, p. 190. [2] *Ibid.*

of the value of practice. Consequently it tends to a gross " fideism[1]."

The philosophy of action, on the other hand, seeks truth as intrinsic to action, maintaining that action includes thought. It does not, therefore, oppose thought to practice but unites them in a living union by accepting the " man entire " with all his powers of knowing, willing, loving, acting. The " philosophy of action " includes, M. Blondel asserts, a " philosophy of the idea." It is thus, he concludes, neither intellectualism nor pragmatism.

Can this conclusion be substantiated ? On the one hand, in the discussion above referred to, M. Parodi maintained that there is " an evident relationship," but the only evidence he adduces in support of the contention, so far as I can discover, is that the " philosophy of action... without attempting to subordinate knowledge to any utilitarian consideration, even in the most exalted sense of the word, believes it possible to establish between thought and life, intelligence and action complex processes of mutual influence, and wishes to conceive truth as something which ought to interest and satisfy the entire man[2]," and from this he concludes that " many ideas of the French philosophy of action are found again in the Anglo-Saxon pragmatists, although in a somewhat troubled confusion, and with ultimate tendencies that are different enough."

Now, it seems to me that this is not sufficient to establish the relationship. It is true that there may be some ideas common to both philosophies, and assuredly the philosophy of action conceives truth as something that must interest and satisfy " the entire man," for this would appear to be true of *all* philosophies except the extreme

[1] *B.S.F.Ph.* 1908, Appendix.   [2] *loc. cit.* p. 265.

intellectualism which is apparently a figment of the pragmatist's brain, and, perhaps, of the pragmatist himself, who, in his extreme anti-intellectualistic ardour, is apt to neglect and scorn the claims of *intellect* even to share in the " satisfaction " that is the mark of truth !

The relationship, then, appears to exist only in their common voluntarism, and here it is important to notice that M. Blondel, and his disciple M. Laberthonnière, go beyond *will* to *love*, which they seem to regard as the perfection alike of will and intellect, of action and knowledge, much in the manner of Dr McTaggart, whom no one would accuse of being a pragmatist !

There is, indeed, it seems to me a more obvious relationship between the conclusions of Dr McTaggart and those of MM. Blondel and Laberthonnière than there is between the latter and pragmatism. Dr McTaggart in his determination of the ultimate nature of the Absolute reaches the conclusion that " If anything in our present lives can resolve the contradictions inherent in knowledge and volition, and exhibit the truth which lies concealed in them, it must be love[1]," for love alone satisfies the threefold test of, absolute balance between the individual and the reality which is for it ; perfect unity between self and not self ; the grounding of the unique nature of each individual in its relations with other individuals. Only love, then, can be the perfect manifestation of the Absolute.

This conclusion, which, as Dr McTaggart says, is " fairly to be called mystical," is in close agreement with the position reached by MM. Laberthonnière and Blondel, and in the case of the former the agreement is striking even in matters of detail. He also conceives the ultimate

---

[1] *Studies in Hegelian Cosmology*, § 283.

reality as a unity of individuals bound together in and through love, in which each is an end to each in the same way as to himself, so that there ceases to be opposition between self and other selves. Moreover, in the concrete unity of life, M. Laberthonnière says, action and knowledge are identical, for both are love—" Love is then the first and the last word of all. It is the principle, the means and the end. It is in loving that one gets away from self and raises oneself above one's temporal individuality. It is in loving that one finds God and other beings and that one finds oneself....And love is at the same time light, heat and life[1]."

I do not, of course, mean to imply that MM. Blondel and Laberthonnière can be designated " Hegelians "— though the title would perhaps be less inept than that of " pragmatists "—but it is clear that for them " action " signifies a transcendence of knowledge and will, which may perhaps be best expressed by the term—which, indeed, M. Laberthonnière employs—" love." Both terms are inadequate, for, as M. Blondel says, their aim is to reserve " to our diverse powers of knowing, of willing, of loving and of acting all their respective parts[2]," and to show " how these elements are solid in the synthesis which reason contributes to form and to justify, but which are fully realised, maintained and perfected only by effective practice." Nevertheless, much of his phraseology suggests, and the whole trend of his argument confirms, the view that the nature of the " living synthesis " is best expressed as love, a love in which the opposition of action and knowledge shall be—as for Dr McTaggart—overcome.

---

[1] *Essais de philosophie religieuse*, p. 110.
[2] *B.S.F.Ph.* 1908, p. 295.

There is a close affinity, it seems to me, between
M. Blondel's philosophy and that of M. Le Roy. The
"action" of which M. Blondel speaks is the "lived-
thought" or "*pensée-action*" of M. Le Roy. It is true that
M. Blondel lays more stress on logical considerations than
does M. Le Roy, and he does not glorify the "obscure" at
the expense of the "clear[1]," nevertheless the tendency
of his philosophy is towards a mysticism that escapes the
limits of clear thinking, and can be expressed only in
symbols.

The philosophy of action approaches, on its religious
side, to the Symbolo-Fideism of Protestant theology as
represented, for example, by Auguste Sabatier and
M. Ménégoz. It has been pointed out that M. Le Roy
attributes to dogmas only a practical sense ; they are rules
of conduct, not theoretical formulae ; their significance
is above all practical and moral, not intellectual ; their
function is rather to exclude errors in conduct than to
determine truth. From the intellectual point of view,
then, a dogma has no positive value, nevertheless, although
"by itself and in itself it (dogma) has only a practical
sense" yet, "a mysterious reality corresponds to it and it
thus places before the intelligence a theoretical problem[2]."
M. Le Roy thus endeavours to safeguard the intellectual
element and to attribute to the dogma *some* value of
knowledge.

The attitude of the Symbolo-Fideist is very similar.
"Religious knowledge," says Sabatier, " is *symbolical*. All

---

[1] The following sentence might well be used to indicate M. Blondel's
meaning : "Par *Action*, il faut entendre la vie spirituelle intégrale, non
pas un mode particulier de vie, le mode irréflechi et obscur." Le Roy in
B.S.F.Ph. 1908, p. 273.

[2] *Dogme et Critique*, p. 33.

the notions it forms and organises...are necessarily inadequate to their object. They are never equivalent, as in the case of the exact sciences[1]." The truths of religion are beyond our comprehension, but they can be revealed in symbols. Knowledge is limited; faith, however, may go beyond knowledge, and in this we may find the meaning of the Fideist formula: "Salvation by faith, independently of beliefs[2]." By "belief" is meant intellectual conviction; by "faith" a "change of heart" that is, above all, an attitude of acceptance, an attitude that is the work not of intellectual persuasion, but of a movement of love.

In so far as the Symbolo-Fideist regards the symbols as merely means to orientate our action, he is pragmatic; in so far as he lays stress on their inadequacy as knowledge, he goes beyond pragmatism, for he attributes a value of knowledge to the symbols and points to a truth that is more than utility.

In its extreme forms, especially as represented by the writers in the Catholic *Revue de philosophie*, Fideism becomes a caricature of Pragmatism and has nothing in common with the "philosophy of action."

4. THE NEO-CRITICISM OF RENOUVIER.

(1) Kant's true successor in France is Renouvier rather than the so-called "French Kant," Maine de Biran. Although, like de Biran, Renouvier starts from the free activity of will, and makes will, in the assertion of its

---

[1] *Outlines of a Philosophy of Religion*, p. 322.

[2] Ménégoz in *Publications diverses sur le Fidéisme*, I. p. 251, and *passim*.

freedom, the first principle of knowledge, he was but slightly, if at all, influenced by the former. While for de Biran free will is a fact given in experience, for Renouvier it rests on a psychological analysis of the act of deliberation and on a study of the concept of cause.

In defining " will " Renouvier is careful to confine it to the sphere of reflective consciousness; he clearly distinguishes—with especial reference to de Biran—the effort involved in willing from muscular effort, or sensation, for the purpose of raising "in another sphere the fact of volition properly so-called, of which biology can discover no sign, nor any fact corresponding in its domain[1]." The will acts only in the sphere of representation and is neither a separate faculty—an entity—nor a struggle of ideas, but a character of the representation itself. " I understand by volition," he says, " the character of an act of consciousness which represents itself not simply as given, but as being able or having been able to be or not to be, excited or continued, without other apparent change than that which is connected with the representation itself in so far as it summons or averts the representation[2]." All volition is effort, and it is this characteristic of effort—itself indefinable—that constitutes a representation voluntary, in contradistinction from a " simple " representation, and " this distinction will be that of thinking and of willing." Its essence is that a voluntary representation "seems to arise without previous efficient cause, that is which seems first to cause itself, then to determine the other representations[3]." Hence, " the will is a principle of the solution of the continuity of phenomena: it does not obey an a priori

[1] *Essais: Deuxième Essai*, I. p. 397.   [2] *Ibid.* I. p. 301.
[3] *Ibid.* I. p. 297.

law." Thus, Renouvier concludes "in defining will, I have
defined liberty[1]." Will is self-caused representation, and
liberty is freedom of will in reflective action, which is
emotional and intellectual as well as volitional. *Pure* will
is as much an abstraction as *pure* intellect; it is the error
of indifferentism and determinism alike to regard the will
as a separable entity, whereas it is indissolubly united to
the intellectual and emotional elements in the human
personality.

According to Renouvier, then, the will is, as such, free.
He admits, however, that "the assertion of freedom is not
logically demonstrable, any more than is that of necessity[2],"
but the balance of probability inclines, he thinks, to the
side of liberty, which is supported by mathematical considerations with regard to the concepts of chance and
infinity, and still more strongly by arguments drawn from
the nature of the moral law. But in thus passing judgment in favour of liberty, free judgment is assumed, and
thus "it is freedom itself which must decide whether
freedom is a fact or not[3]." How then can certainty on
this question be attained? This raises the question of
the nature of certainty itself which Renouvier held to be
grounded in liberty, hence "the problem of freedom is
posited even in the fact of the solution given to it, hence
we see how freedom and truth are bound up together[4]."

By certainty Renouvier means the contrary of doubt,
and there are, he holds, three cases in which one does not
doubt, viz. "when one *sees*, when one *knows*, when one
believes[5]." Belief seems the weakest of these because we
use it when we are not certain, but on analysis we find,

---

[1] *Essais: Deuxième Essai*, I. p. 306. [2] *Ibid.* II. p. 89.
[3] *Ibid.* II. p. 92. [4] *Ibid.* II. p. 93. [5] *Ibid.* II. p. 130.

Renouvier says, that, since we are always liable to error, we do not *know* but only *believe* we know, and thus "it would seem that of the three terms, that of belief is the most general and includes the two others. We ought to say that *we believe we see*, that we *believe we know*, and always that *we believe*."

This prevalence of doubt—for all belief is founded on preliminary doubt—is the supreme characteristic of man, that which makes him distinctively *human* and enlightened, whereas "the ignorant doubts little, the drunkard still less, and the madman never[1]."

Belief is thus a genus which includes "seeing" and "knowing." Knowledge has, then, no greater certainty than Belief. Renouvier's purpose seems to be to raise Belief to the status of Knowledge, rather than to degrade Knowledge to Belief. Yet, he is forced to recognise a distinction between them that constitutes a difference *in kind*, for he says we should say we *know* that we believe. This view is summed up finally in a sentence quoted from Jules Lequier, where he says "when one believes with the firmest faith that one possesses truth, one ought to know that one believes it, not believe that one knows it[2]." Here, then, knowledge appears as superior in certainty to belief.

Why then does Renouvier ascribe greater certainty to belief? It is the consequence of his view that in all affirmation the will enters as factor. He recognises two "orders of certainty," and although the second order will be "characterised by the greater place that doubt, the passions and the will occupy in the human establishment

[1] *Essais: Deuxième Essai*, II. p. 152.
[2] *Ibid.* II. p. 195.

of truth[1]," yet even the "first order" is not exempt from
doubt, and thus "every affirmation in which consciousness
is reflective is subordinated, in consciousness, to the determination to affirm." Affirmation is, therefore, *determination*
to affirm, hence belief.

Thus arises the importance of the question "are we
free in our inmost consciousness, or are we predestined to
believe, to affirm, to deny, to doubt?" It is in the answer
to this question that we shall find the "first truth," and
the foundation of certainty.

In the investigation of this problem Renouvier was
profoundly influenced by his friend Jules Lequier, fragments of whose works he published as appendices to the
chapters of the second edition of his *Essais de Critique
Général* in order to show his indebtedness to the com-
paratively unknown philosopher, whose method of dealing
with the problem he adopted, describing it as "Lequier's
dilemma." The statement that follows is based upon that
of Lequier.

It is in the nature of a first truth to be indemonstrable,
for all demonstration is deductive, hence requires evidence,
or pre-existing truth. To set out from universal doubt,
will must be substituted for evidence in order to create
belief. The Cartesian formula, Lequier held, affords no
starting point; setting out from "*cogito*" there is no bridge
to "*sum.*" To pass from doubt there must be evidence or
will. Evidence is here inadmissible, for, since all evidence
is deductive it requires a preexisting truth. But "universal
doubt" sweeps away all basis for deductive synthetic
argument. On the one hand is "*moi-pensée,*" on the other
"*moi-objet.*" To bridge the gap we need a "*moi-volonté*"

[1] *Essais: Deuxième Essai,* II. p. 321.

which unites the two selves into a complete self—"*moi-vivant.*" In this free act of will is found the first truth that guarantees the passage from "*cogito*" to "*sum.*" Because this bond is necessary for the affirmation of the self, I affirm myself in order to produce it. Thus will is necessary to affirm the existence of the self by a synthetic judgment which unites the thinking self to the object self. This synthetic judgment is an act of free will, a belief. Doubt is, then, replaced by belief.

This belief, since it is a first truth, cannot be demonstrated, but must be postulated, and must be postulated *freely.*—"In the impossibility of demonstrating anything, the sole resource that remains is to affirm liberty by right of a postulate[1]." Formulate, then, the possible alternatives, and the result is the dilemma—Necessity necessarily, or freely, affirmed; liberty necessarily, or freely, affirmed. We must then "choose between the one and the other with the one or with the other[2]." If we examine the alternatives we see that (*a*) necessity necessarily affirmed gives us no guarantee as to its reality, since the contradictory affirmation is equally necessary; (*b*) necessity freely affirmed does not exclude doubt, since it is, in this case as in the other, necessity that is affirmed; (*c*) liberty necessarily affirmed still affords no escape from doubt, but it has an advantage over the first two cases since it admits a basis for morals; (*d*) liberty freely affirmed supplies, not only a basis for morals, but a guarantee of truth. It follows, then, that the affirmation of necessity involves contradiction, since it cannot be denied that some affirm liberty, which, if the necessitarian doctrine be true, they do necessarily. The affirmation of liberty, on the other hand, does not involve

[1] *Ibid.* II. p. 417.   [2] *Ibid.* II. p. 421.

a like absurdity. Its position is thus of superior practical value. The conclusion drawn is " We ought then to choose it (liberty) and to determine ourselves to it, if we remember that here is logically a case of doubt, as we have shown, and which is further proved by the use of a mode of reasoning such as the dilemma in order to escape from doubt ; it is a case in which belief is unavoidable whatever side we take[1]."

But there are not lacking logical reasons to incline us to this belief, for Renouvier points out that " the profound consideration of error and of truth, of their possibility and of their nature adduces powerful reasons in favour of that one of the two which explains things most humanly[2]."

If necessity be true, then there is no distinction between error and truth, since in the case of divergent opinions both are necessitated, hence could not be otherwise. Thus error is as necessary as truth, and in one sense must cease to be error.

If, however, liberty be true, then error results from judgments which need not have been formed and have thus "nothing fatalistic about them." In admitting the possibility of real alternatives, room is made for error.

It is true that in neither case do we obtain any criterion of truth, but, whereas in the system of necessity the lack of criterion is due to lack of the distinction itself, in the system of liberty we should expect to find no criterion, for that would impose constraint, and we should be *forced* to affirm. While, then, we shall not always avoid error, we shall always be *able* to avoid it. The essence of the method is the exercise of liberty itself, so that " we make error and truth in ourselves, putting ourselves, after free examination, into contradiction or agreement with external realities the affirmation of which is not necessarily imposed upon consciousness[1]."

To sum up then in Lequier's words, quoted by Renouvier, " I refuse to follow the work of a knowledge *which would not be mine*. I accept the *certainty of which I am the author*," hence, he adds, " I have found the first truth which I sought," viz.—"liberty, the positive condition of knowledge and the means of knowledge[2]."

The first truth is, then, a free and individual act of faith. Only in so far as we are conscious of freedom can we attain philosophic certainty. This theory was generalised by Renouvier to cover the whole of philosophy, and it is significant that, once adopted, the 'principle of Lequier' constrains him to sum up all philosophical problems in a series of dilemmas between which choice must, he says, be made. Since each side of the dilemmas is reduced to a logical unity, we may sum up the ultimate metaphysical alternative—" Is there only a natural order, or is there also a moral order to which the natural order is subordinated ? " In other words—" Is the moral order supreme ? " The answer to this question, Renouvier holds, we cannot *know*, we can only believe. But we must answer one way or the other; that is, we make a " moral wager." We thus come to the position of " Pascal's wager," and a consideration of this may make clear the relation of Renouvier to present day Pragmatism.

It is with direct reference to Pascal that Renouvier speaks of a moral wager. His objection to Pascal's wager is due to its content—belief in the Catholic faith—not to its form. Stated in Pascal's terms, Renouvier is not willing

[1] *Ibid.* II. p. 349.   [2] *Ibid.* II. p. 422.

to admit "you must wager; that is not within your own power, you are committed to it[1]." A wager that involves belief in the Catholic faith is not—to use an expression of James'—a "living option" to Renouvier.

But the method of the wager he recognises as correct, and himself applies it to the question as to the existence or non-existence of a moral order. In this form, he says, "it is logically unassailable because of the scope it leaves for the definition of the alternatives[2]."

It is interesting to note, then, James' own treatment of Pascal's wager. Having baldly stated it, James concludes "When religious faith expresses itself thus, in the language of the gaming table, it is put to its last trumps[3]." To show the absurdity of such a method he asks what appeal would such a wager make if for the Catholic faith we were to substitute belief in the Mahdi. Hence, he adds, that from this point of view, the attempt to believe by our volition is "worse than silly, it is vile[4]."

Nevertheless, a few pages farther on we find that there are cases when "Pascal's argument, instead of being powerless" becomes "a regular clincher, and is the last stroke needed to make our faith in masses and holy water complete[5]."

These cases are—as we should suspect—those in which the option is not only forced, but the hypotheses, which form the terms of the option, are "living." It is again, then, not Pascal's method that is refused, but the *terms* of his wager. State the wager in terms that offer a living

[1] Pascal, *Pensées*, Ed. Brunschvicg, Vol. II. p. 146.
[2] *La Nouvelle Monadologie*, p. 458.
[3] *The Will to Believe*, p. 6.   [4] *op. cit.* p. 7.
[5] *op. cit.* p. 11.

option to the will, and "Pascal's logic" becomes "a regular clincher"!

This point seems to me of great importance because it brings out clearly the pragmatic position which is precisely that of Pascal's wager, the determining factor being interest or utility as source of the "force" of the option. It is summed up by James in the thesis: "Our passional nature not only lawfully may, but must, decide an option between propositions, whenever it is a genuine option that cannot be decided on intellectual grounds[1]." His condemnation of Pascal's wager seems to me, then, extremely inconsistent and indefensible.

This also would appear to be the position of Renouvier, and in his *Deuxième Essai*, where the influence of Lequier dominates, in dealing with the problem of certainty Renouvier based truth on will or free affirmation. It must be remembered, however, that, throughout his treatment of the dilemmas between which choice is to be made, Renouvier himself invokes reasons logically justifiable, and asserts that the thesis of liberty involves "ni difficultés insurmountables ni contradiction," whereas "au contraire, les doctrines qui posent la nécessité se heurtent d'ordinaire à la contradiction de l'infini actuel[2]." Not only does he not share James' aversion to logic but he makes appeal to it, and is the author of the "First Essay" on Logic, no less than of the "Second," on Psychology.

Nevertheless, many of the criticisms directed against Pragmatism are valid against Renouvier, and it may be that his influence on James tended towards the pragmatism of the latter.

A consideration of the exact relation of Renouvier's

[1] *Ibid.*   [2] *op. cit.* II. p. 89.

theory of certainty to Kant's second critique would perhaps not only make clear the precise relation between Renouvier and James, but would also aid in determining how far Pragmatism may be regarded as a development from Kantian "Voluntarism."

Before considering this, we may examine the part assigned by Renouvier to will in the establishing of truth. There must, he says, be freedom of will, since otherwise error would be as necessary as truth, and "error is then truth, because necessary, and the true can become false. Madness has against it only its weakness, and erroneous opinions only their inconsistency[1]." (We may note in passing that Renouvier seems to think that the *inconsistency* of erroneous opinions constitutes no essential distinction between them and true opinions.)

He argues, then, that since error and truth *are* distinguished, there must be liberty of will; but if in all judgment free decision is possible, then doubt is possible; hence doubt may extend to all judgments and the only way to escape scepticism is by *willing* to affirm a judgment, and that affirmation will be free belief.

It may be granted that we cannot set out from the circle of doubt without the aid of will, and that consequently will is an element in all affirmation. But this does not involve the conclusion that will *makes* truth. We will *that*, and not *what*, the judgment may be. Hence *what* is true is independent of our willing, though *that* it is true may result from our action.

Renouvier's attempt to make knowledge identical with belief, with the purpose of raising belief to the status of

[1] *op. cit.* II. p. 59.

postulates may enable us to define more clearly their mutual relations.

(i) While it must be admitted that Pragmatism can be regarded as a development from Kant, it is, I think, a one-sided development that neglects more essential elements, and overlooks the limitations imposed by Kant on postulation and his caution in ascribing objective truth to the postulates demanded by practical reason. The " attitude of the will " is, in each case, entirely different.

Kant's much quoted phrase—" I must therefore abolish knowledge to make room for belief "—makes a distinction between *knowledge* and *belief* that is wholly obliterated in Pragmatism. Thus Kant admits postulation only where knowledge fails, and such postulates give only belief. " The postulates of pure practical reason are not," he says, " theoretical dogmas, but presuppositions that are practically necessary. They do not enlarge our speculative knowledge, but give objective reality to the ideas of speculative reason in general, and justify it in the use of conceptions which it could not otherwise venture to regard as even possible[1]." As he elsewhere points out, this *moral belief* or conviction " is not a *logical* but a *moral* certainty ; and, as it rests on subjective grounds (of the moral sentiment), I must not even say that *it is* morally certain that there is a God, etc., but that *I* am morally certain, etc. What I really mean is," he goes on to say, " that the belief in a God and in another world is so interwoven with my moral sentiment, that there is as little danger of my losing the latter, as there is any fear lest I should ever be deprived of the former[2]."

[1] *Crit. of Pract. Reason* (Trans. Watson).
[2] *Crit. of Pure Reason* (M. Müller's Trans.), ii. p. 711.

In this connection Kant distinguishes three degrees of certainty—(a) *Trowing*, when the evidence is insufficient both subjectively and objectively; (b) *Believing*, when evidence is sufficient subjectively, insufficient objectively; (c) *Knowing*, when the evidence is sufficient subjectively and objectively, and this last gives *certainty* for everybody, whereas believing, he says, gives only conviction for myself. It is clear that the postulates of practical reason fall into the second class, but because they are inseparably bound up with the conception of duty, the *belief* they give rises to the level of *moral certainty*, hence are not unstable and subject to revision as *mere belief* is.

The recognition of a voluntary element in the postulates is brought out very clearly in the *Critique of Practical Reason*, but Kant is most careful to restrict its scope, for postulation must not be "for the sake of an arbitrary speculative purpose, but of a practically necessary end of a pure rational will, which in this case does not *choose*, but *obeys* an inexorable command of reason, the foundation of which is *objective*, in the constitution of things as they must be universally judged by pure reason, and is not based on *inclination*[1]." The moral law being taken as binding, the man who recognises this has a right to say, "I *will* that there be a God, that my existence in this world be also an existence outside the chain of physical causes, and, lastly, that my duration be endless."

There is an element of choice in that only those who recognise the obligation of the moral law, and will it, can postulate God, Freedom, Immortality, and these three postulates are, for them, *practically* necessary because needed to complete the moral law, while they are not

[1] *op. cit.* Bk. II. c. 2.

in contradiction with pure speculative reason, although they transcend it.

Postulation, then, is an integral part of Kant's critical philosophy; it may even be said to be the goal he set before him, if the first critique be regarded as clearing the way, by mainly negative conclusions, to " make room for belief."

But between Kant's standpoint and the pragmatist's there is a wide gulf. Firstly, as we have already noted, Kant admits postulation only when knowledge fails, thus establishing a distinction between them. Secondly, he restricts postulation to the three objects demanded by the moral law. Thirdly, he says that the postulates cannot be verified because here knowledge is impossible, but the pragmatist says the postulates are verified if they " *work*," and then they *become* knowledge.

It seems to me, then, that the nature of Kant's postulation is fundamentally different from its use in Pragmatism. Dr Schiller, however, in dealing with the postulate, makes direct appeal to the authority of Kant. If we take the standpoint of Kant's Practical Reason, he argues, we are forced to go the whole length of *Axioms as Postulates*. " Postulation," he says, " cannot be confined to ethics. The principle, if valid, must be generalised and applied all round to the organising principles of our life," and, again, " postulation is either not valid at all or it is the foundation of the whole theoretic superstructure[1]."

It is difficult to see the force of this " must," but perhaps, in laying the foundations of Pragmatism, Dr Schiller disdains appeals to logic! In any case, it does not seem to me an extension of a Kantian principle, but a

[1] *Personal Idealism*, p. 90.

denial of it. Kant's postulates are inseparably bound up with the demands of the moral law which necessitates belief in God, Freedom, Immortality, and this belief is not *opposed* to knowledge, but goes beyond the limits of knowledge. In saying, therefore, as Dr Schiller does, that " we cannot *act as if* the existence of God, Freedom, and Immortality were real, if at the same time we *know* that it is hopelessly inaccessible and indemonstrable[1]," he seems to me deliberately to imply that Kant held that this belief was " believing what you know isn't true," whereas it is quite clear that Kant meant that we do *not* know it to be *un*true, but that its truth cannot be demonstrated to the satisfaction of the speculative reason, but can be held as true in the light of the Practical Reason. As Kant himself put it, we have *moral* certainty, not *logical.*

Indeed, Dr Schiller's whole treatment of the relation between Kant's two critiques seems to me to be based on a fundamental misconception, when he says that Kant, having become " partly and tardily aware of the fatal error of his intellectualism and of the impossibility of accommodating the whole of life on the basis prescribed by the *Critique of Pure Reason*[2]," proceeded to make up the deficiency by the reckless assumption of the principle of postulation. It appears to me quite evident that Kant had in view from the first some such treatment as is found in the second critique, and that it is distinctly foreshadowed in such a passage as the following, which occurs in the *Critique of Pure Reason* (both in the first and second editions) :—" Reason in its purely speculative use is quite incapable of proving the existence of a Supreme Being. At the same time it is of very great value in this way,

[1] *Personal Idealism*, p. 89.　　　　[2] *Ibid*. p. 87.

that it is able to *correct* our knowledge of that Being, should it be possible to obtain a knowledge of it in any other way[1]."

We conclude, then, that Kant's use of postulation was not an afterthought, nor is there any need that the first critique " be re-written in the light of the principle of the Postulate[2]."

Pragmatism, on the other hand, illegitimately generalises postulation to cover the whole ground of knowledge.

(ii) Renouvier, himself, summing up his relation to Kant, claims that he has modified Kant's doctrine in three important respects :—(*a*) by including all the categories under the " Law of Relation " which leads to denial of the noumenon ; (*b*) by his doctrine of liberty, from which, he says, follow many logical conclusions opposed to Kant ; (*c*) by his critique of Infinity[3].

The first and third points, which are worked out in the First Essay of the *Essais de Critique Générale*, establish his Neo-criticism under the influence of the Kantian critical philosophy. The second point, his doctrine of liberty, is first fully worked out in the *Deuxième Essai* of the series, in which the influence of Jules Lequier predominates, so it seems to me, to the entire exclusion of Kant, although the Essai is entitled *Traité de Psychologie rationnelle d'après les Principes du criticisme.*

It is his doctrine of liberty that determines his theory of certainty, hence it is of the greatest importance for our present purpose to examine the exact way in which Renouvier makes use of postulation.

For Renouvier, as for Kant, the supreme interest of

---

[1] *op. cit.* 1st Ed. p. 639.   [2] Schiller in *op. cit.* p. 90.
[3] *Philos. Analytic*, IV. pp. 432 *seq.*

philosophy is in relation to the moral nature of man. It is his conviction that the distinction between right and wrong no less than that between truth and error would be abolished were man not free, that weighs so strongly with him and leads him to proclaim human freedom. He thus agrees with Kant in recognising the connection of moral obligation with freedom, but, in denying the noumenal world, he brings freedom into the world of phenomena. Further, since man is free, he cannot be constrained to accept truth, unless this truth be his own work ; otherwise necessity would be reinstated. All philosophical problems can, therefore, as we have seen, be stated in the form of a dilemma, either side of which may be freely chosen, since there is no constraining reason to determine the choice. Thus we reach the principle of the " moral wager " already discussed.

Now it seems to me that in his doctrine of liberty, and in the consequences that flow from it, the standpoint of Renouvier is fundamentally different from Kant's, and that it is just at this point that a transition is made possible from the doctrine of the Practical Reason to Pragmatism. It is, then, I think, possible to hold that Renouvier constitutes the link between Kant and e.g. James, while, on the other hand, it seems an exaggeration to describe Renouvier as a " pragmatist " if that be taken to mean essentially belief in the equivalence of truth and utility.

How wide the divergence is between Renouvier and Kant at this point may be estimated by a consideration of the principle involved in deciding truth by means of a moral wager. This may, I think, be fairly done, since Renouvier expressly defends the *method* of " Pascal's

Wager," though objecting to the terms in which Pascal originally formulated it[1]. The chances, then, of either side of a given dilemma being true are assumed to be equal. A bet must be made. But one of the alternatives is preferable, i.e. it appeals to some interest other than intellectual. This interest determines on which side the stake is to be placed, and the bet is made. The result gives, according to Renouvier, belief in one of the alternatives, and this belief constitutes the highest grade of certainty to which we can attain. In other words *belief* is raised to the status of *knowledge*. We are free to postulate, and our postulation carries with it certainty; it gives us knowledge. This postulation is extended over the whole ground of philosophy.

In this connection it is interesting to note that Kant mentions a kind of belief which he calls "doctrinal belief," the proper method of testing which is, he says, "by means of a bet[2]." The bet will prove with how great a degree of conviction the belief is held. It may be, he says, a belief valued at one ducat, but not at ten ; and so on. "If," he says, "I should be ready to stake the whole of my earthly goods on my belief," then it is shown to be "not only an opinion, but a strong belief," but it never rises to the level of knowledge, hence is always unstable. But he goes on to show that such belief is quite different from *moral belief* which leads me to postulate what is essential to the moral law. Even here, however, belief does not rise to knowledge, but the belief itself is objectively necessary, provided that I recognise the moral law. In this case the

---

[1] *Esquisse d'une Classif. Sys. des doctr. phil.* II. pp. 50—58 and pp. 300—324. And *La Nouvelle Monadologie.*

[2] *Critique of Pure Reason*, chapter on "The Canon of Pure Reason."

belief is *unshakable*, and gives *moral* certainty. Moreover, such postulation is only valid where the moral law demands it; hence it cannot be used to solve the antinomies within the pure reason itself. But this, of course, is just what Renouvier does.

Apart from any other objections that may be urged, it seems to me that the method is essentially unsatisfactory, since the antinomies—or dilemmas—are antinomies of *reason*, hence an extra-rational method of solving them does not, from the point of view of reason, offer a solution at all[1]. Indeed, Renouvier's attempt to replace knowledge by belief—transferring the certainty of the former to the latter—seems to me to end in reducing all knowledge to the unstable condition of belief, and to abandon the attempt to solve problems put by reason.

While, however, there is a resemblance between the method of postulation as used by Renouvier and by the pragmatists, their adoption of the method appears to be approached from different points of view.

Renouvier's doctrine of liberty leads him to renounce all constraint, even the constraint of truth. He is thereby enabled to account for the existence of error. But he claims a logical, as well as a psychological, foundation for his *méthode dichotomique*, viz., the impossibility of demonstrating first principles. Even the principle of contradiction cannot be demonstrated without *petitio principii*, and this, he says, is "an unmistakeable sign of the impossibility of giving to metaphysics a foundation which requires for its establishment nothing from the practical factors of the usage of reason[2]."

[1] See infra, p. 162.
[2] *Dilemmes de la mét. pure*, p. 256.

It is quite obvious that it was for no such reason that Kant resorted to postulates.

There are apparently two causes which lead the pragmatist to adopt the method of postulation. Firstly, he wishes to recognise the "purposive character of human thought," and give full weight to the emotional and volitional aspect of human nature. Secondly, he wishes to extend the experimental method of science to metaphysic, and in so doing he transforms the "hypothesis" into the "postulate." The postulate will be proved by the way it "works," and its truth will be simply its utility.

It may well be doubted whether Renouvier would have concurred in the view that the "real world" is the result of our experimenting; and it is, I think, quite certain that he would not have admitted that truth *means* utility, or that knowledge has only an instrumental value.

If, then, these two latter statements be admitted to constitute the essence of Pragmatism, then, it appears to be incorrect to describe Renouvier as a pragmatist.

On the other hand, his use of the moral wager, hence his postulation, and his theory of certainty show some affinity with Pragmatism. Even here, however, in admitting non-intellectual factors in the determination of truth, Renouvier seeks to exclude all considerations of "interest" that are not derived from moral motives[1]. This limitation, however, leaves over the difficulty of defining *how much* is to be included in "interest," and leaves room for the pragmatist to supply the deficiency with "emotional" and "utilitarian" considerations.

To sum up. While Renouvier cannot, strictly speaking, be called a pragmatist, nevertheless he forms a link between

[1] *Classif.* II. p. 297.

Kant and the pragmatists, and through him a line of development may be traced from the *Critique of Practical Reason* to Dr Schiller's *Axioms as Postulates* and the *Experimental Theory of Knowledge* of Prof. Dewey. But on the way, essential elements have been dropped out, and the development is both one-sided and illogical.

In the development of French Voluntarism, Renouvier alone shows any affinity with Anglo-American Pragmatism.

5. THE "PHILOSOPHIE DES IDÉES-FORCES."

(1) The tendency to disparage intellect that we found to be the most marked characteristic of contemporary philosophy is common to writers of very different schools, and the general term " anti-intellectualism "—made current chiefly by pragmatists—not only conceals differences as vital as any point of agreement, but is so ambiguous as to be practically useless as a label. The negative title seems to have been adopted mainly for the purpose of marking hostility to Mr Bradley, but in his case, at least, the contrary title " intellectualist " is singularly inept and misleading.

The less ambiguous term " Voluntarism[1] " may, however, be more fitly used to denote generally those philosophers who agree, not only in their revolt against excessive intellectualism, but also in their tendency to conceive the

[1] I am, however, glad to see that recently a protest has been made by Prof. Dawes Hicks " against the debasing of the philosophical currency by the coinage of misleading and really meaningless epithets like 'intellectualism' and 'voluntarism.'" And he goes on to quote from Mr Russell the remark that an intellectualist "is anyone who is not a pragmatist," adding, "and that, I suppose, is what it comes to." But none of the French Voluntarists fall under either designation.

(In a paper read before the Aristotelian Society in November 1912.)

ultimate nature of reality as some form of will, hence to lay stress on activity as the main feature of experience, and to base their philosophy upon the psychological fact of the immediate consciousness of volitional activity. It is this recognition of, and emphasis on, the reality and efficacy of volitional activity that, starting from Maine de Biran, links together the line of French philosophy represented by Ravaisson, Renouvier, Boutroux, Poincaré, Fouillée, Bergson, Le Roy and Wilbois, in spite of wide divergences in method and conclusions.

Nevertheless, although M. Fouillée may be rightly classed with de Biran and the line of philosophy developed from him, yet he stands out somewhat from the main line, and I think it is extremely doubtful whether he would accept the title "anti-intellectualist." A more appropriate title for his philosophy would be, I think, "Intellectualistic Voluntarism[1]"—if the apparent verbal contradiction may be allowed. The most prominent feature of his philosophy seems to me his attempt to reconcile the voluntaristic and intellectualistic aspects of mind, to deny that water-tight compartments can be established between "appetite" and intellect, and to insist upon the indissoluble connection between "idea" and "will." Although will is fundamental it does not exist in isolation; it is not separable from intelligence and feeling. We do not, he says, "vouloir à *vide*"; there is always an object of will and "this object is always revealed to us by sensation, and its relation to our will is always manifested by painful or agreeable

[1] Since the above was written M. Fouillée's last work—*La Pensée et les Nouvelles Ecoles Anti-intellectualistes*—has been published, and in it he definitely adopts the term "*Volontarisme intellectualiste*" to denote his own doctrine.

feeling." Hence, "the law of the mental reflex, with its three moments, is then the law of the will, which, having become conscious, binds with an unbreakable link these three terms: motive, impulse, determination[1]."

M. Fouillée uses the term "idea" in the Cartesian sense, as equivalent to the whole state of consciousness in so far as it is inseparable from some representation. The idea as "pure idea," or mere intellection, he considers an abstraction. It is the mistake of intellectualism to regard ideas under a statical aspect, as pictures, that is as purely representative. But mental phenomena are primarily *appetitions* which only later become representations. At first the living being seeks only adaptation to environment; it is later that ideas are regarded as representative of the objects to which adaptation is necessary. For ideas as "representations," then, the psychology of "idées-forces" must substitute ideas as "*forms of will.*" Its fundamental principle is the recognition of every conscious state as a process constituted by three inseparable terms— (*a*) a *discernment* which makes changes of state felt, and is the germ of sensation and intellect; (*b*) pleasure or pain which causes reaction to the change of state; (*c*) active movement which is the germ of preference, i.e. of appetition. When this threefold process reaches the reflective state "we call it, in the Cartesian and Spinozistic sense, an *idea*, that is a *discernment* inseparable from a preference[2]."

Every conscious state is thus 'idea' in so far as it is apprehension, 'force' in so far as it involves preference as the result of feeling. Preference involves willing, hence every conscious state is essentially appetitive. Fouillée

[1] *Evol. des I.-f.* p. 90.   [2] *Ps. des I.-f.* I. p. ix.

accordingly defines psychology as " *l'étude de la volonté,*" for, he says, "the problem is no longer simply : does there exist a subject ? but, how does it act ? The relation of the subject to its object is no longer a simple relation of representation, but of adaptation and of immanent finality, originally unreflective and irrational[1]."

M. Fouillée works out in detail the implications of will as the fundamental element in psychical life, exhibiting not only sensation and memory but also the higher intellectual processes of conception as forms of appetite. This is an attempt to rewrite psychology from the point of view of Voluntarism.

The two distinguishing characteristics of M. Fouillée's philosophy are his method of conciliation and his theory of " Idées-forces," which are closely connected, since it is by means of the latter that the conciliation between diverse metaphysical theories is to be brought about.

The aim of M. Fouillée is to reconcile contradictory systems of philosophy by means of a " Synthesism " which shall unite the partial truths of each into a single, organic whole. For this end he adopts a " method of conciliation," the main feature of which is the intercalation of mean terms so as to lessen the divergence of the contradictory systems and bring about an increasing approximation between them.

This method was first expounded in the *Revue philosophique* of 1879, and was then set forth in his *L'Avenir de la Métaphysique* (1889). But its first application is found in his earliest important work *La Liberté et le Déterminisme* (published in 1872), where he attempts to reconcile liberty and determinism, and a second application

[1] *Ps. des I.-f.* I. p. xxi.

in *L'Idée moderne du Droit* in the sphere of ethics (published in 1878).

In the earlier work the dominant conception of M. Fouillée's philosophy takes shape as the directing power of the idea of liberty. Here, in dealing with the problem of human freedom, which is, he says, *the* philosophic problem par excellence, he formulated the theory of "idées-forces" which he afterwards worked out in psychology, ethics, sociology and metaphysics. Its most comprehensive statement is to be found in *L'Evolutionnisme des Idées-forces* (1890) which ranks with the *Psychologie des Idées-forces* (1893) as his most important work.

The purpose of the philosophy of " idées-forces " is to establish the principles of a monistic evolution that is at once immanent and experimental. There are, Fouillée says, two classes of facts of which we have positive knowledge : on the one hand, movement, its modes and laws ; on the other, consciousness, its modes and laws. The question is whether the distinction between these is ultimate. Fouillée maintains that it is not, for the conception of will as the fundamental form of psychical life involves the recognition of a psychical element in natural forces, hence the functional unity of the mental and physical. By recognising the indissoluble unity of the mental and physical " we shall have a theory of the ideal that is *immanent* and not transcendent, which will be susceptible of positive verification, since we start neither from the sphere of consciousness, nor from the sphere of nature[1]." Further, this immanent monism is experimental because it is worked out in experience which gives the world as a

[1] *Rv. phil.* 1879, p. 4.

dynamical whole in which mental and physical factors are indissolubly bound together.

The philosophy of "*Idées-forces*" thus leads us to the recognition of a process analogous to appetition in the physical world. Science presupposes a bond between subject and object, and metaphysics seeks this bond in a psychical germ of sensation or appetition in matter. In *L'Evolutionnisme des Idées-forces*, M. Fouillée discusses the question: Is the psychical a real factor? He endeavours to show that the elimination of the psychical factor is a philosophical impossibility. Mechanical evolution, as conceived, for example, by Spencer, is not a cause, but a result; it presupposes an internal evolution which is the result of a real process of appetition.

The mechanical conception of the world, without the psychical element, is purely algebraical. It is the condition of our spatial and temporal representation of phenomena, that is, of their intelligibility to us, but it does not penetrate to the ultimate reality which is living and dynamical. Mechanical evolution hypostasises that part only of our experience that is reducible to mechanism. But evolution is not a law, but a result of laws; it is the form and sign of an appetitive process. The psychical cannot, therefore, be regarded as an "aspect" of the physical, but as making with it the one reality. Hence there is but one evolution, the evolution of the "*Idées-forces*," in which the psychical element—the idea—is conceived dynamically as a force. Thus the force of the idea is "the consciousness itself of the acting reality, which is of an appetitive and perceptive nature, and is consequently mental[1]."

The conception of "*Idées-forces*" is essential to

[1] *Evol. des I.-f.* p. xv.

M. Fouillée's method of conciliation, for it is the various "idées-forces" which supply the necessary "termes moyens" to be intercalated between contradictory systems. This method receives its most important exemplification with regard to the problem of free will, and as this is for our purpose the most important, it will be sufficient to consider its application in this case.

With regard to the question of free will, M. Fouillée appears in marked contrast to other French Voluntarists. He alone stands out as an adherent of determinism, and, to judge by his controversies with M. Renouvier, as the implacable adversary of indeterminism, or free will.

That Voluntarism is not necessarily coupled with freedom of will is evidenced by Schopenhauer, but it must be remembered that he regarded the will in itself as free, and only its phenomenal manifestations as determined.

The emphasis given to freedom as the characteristic of volitional activity is strongly marked by the founder of French Voluntarism—de Biran—and in its latest development in the philosophy of M. Bergson it is no less evident. In estimating M. Fouillée's position it is, then, of importance to determine his attitude with regard to this question. We shall find I think that the divergence is less marked than at first appears, and that, in spite of M. Fouillée's profession of determinism his final position approximates to that of M. Bergson, whose celebrated discussion of free will ends, it seems to me, in a doctrine of self-determination which it is not less hard to differentiate from "soft determinism" than any of the other varieties that have been offered in solution of the problem.

As we have pointed out, M. Fouillée attempts to solve the problem by means of the conception of ideas as forces.

The idea is correlated with movement. Thus Fouillée says "every idea is, in fact, accompanied by a movement and is a restrained action, a movement suspended and maintained at the molecular state: every idea is at the same time a *force*[1]." Every idea, then, contains an active element which, on its physical side, is a force. Hence it corresponds, not only to what has been and is, but to what will be. Volition consists in the determination of an act by an idea of a thing which will result from us and will result only from our action, i.e. by our desire. The idea of the volition enters into the volition itself. Hence ideas may be *motives*, and the idea of liberty itself becomes a force for the realisation of the idea.

The problem is one of causality,—Can we act as a cause in a world of causal relation? Can a being subject to physical laws be morally free? The solution is found by admitting the force of the idea as a determining causal factor. Admitting, as the determinist does, the fact of deliberation, i.e. the conflict of motives, then "among these motives...must be placed the idea of freedom, which here assumes this form: the idea of the directing power of ideas, consequently of the efficacious power of deliberation itself[2]." The mean term is, therefore, found and we have "determinism rectified by the idea of freedom." M. Fouillée has, then, found the conciliation he sought.

Now, it seems to me that this "rectified determinism" does not differ essentially from Prof. Bergson's view of freedom. He admits that free actions are exceptional, being the outcome of the 'deep-seated' ego which lies beneath the social ego of everyday life. Where an action is free it is because "the relation of this action to the state

[1] *Lib. et Dét.* p. 162. [2] *Ibid.* p. 27.

from which it issued could not be expressed by a law, this psychical state being unique of its kind and unable ever to occur again[1]." But it is certainly not essential to M. Fouillée's conception of determinism that conscious states should be capable of repetition, but only that our acts should be considered as a relation between terms, and this binding relation " is not properly necessitated, that is purely determined; it is not any more arbitrary indifference, that is to say purely undetermined: it ought to be conceived as something independent which *determines itself*[2]."

In M. Bergson's conception it appears to me that causality is, to the same extent, involved when he says " it is from the whole soul, in fact, that the free decision springs[3]," thus summing up freedom as a manifestation of the whole personality. This is not to deny that every event must have a cause, but only that *some* events are incapable of repetition, hence cannot be empirically tested by invariable concomitance.

It is interesting to note that M. Bergson—in the sole passage in his writings where he refers to M. Fouillée—criticises the latter's use of the idea of freedom as a counterbalancing motive, because, he says, it involves an appeal to *motives*, i.e. to the associationist psychology of juxtaposed states. But M. Bergson himself admits the influence of motives in the case of the majority of our actions, denying it only in cases of rare moral crises, where the whole personality is involved.

Apart from the difficulties involved in the conception

[1] *D.I.C.* p. 184 (E. Tr. p. 239).
[2] Fouillée, *op. cit.* p. 197 (italics are Fouillée's).
[3] Bergson, *op. cit.* p. 128 (E. Tr. p. 167).

of a fundamental self and a superficial self thus radically diverse, it seems to me that M. Bergson's solution of the question does not go beyond M. Fouillée's; that, in both cases, it amounts to denying the applicability of the law of causation, as understood in the physical world, to conscious volitions which, although determined, are *self*-determined, being the outcome of the whole personality which *is* ourselves.

I have dealt at length with the treatment of this problem because some recognition of freedom would seem to be indispensable to any philosophical system that makes will ultimate. Determinism seems essentially an intellectualist product and comes from regarding the will as less fundamental[1]. Causation essentially involves, it seems to me, the relation of part to whole, and it is because intellectualism regards will as mere adjunct that it considers it to be determined. If, however, will be the whole, it cannot be other than self-determined. Necessity can only exist within the will itself, and this is self-determination.

Now it seems to me that any consistent voluntarism must recognise the freedom of self-determination, and this comes out clearly, I think, in the case of Schopenhauer, who might, at first sight, be cited in disproof. The will in itself, he admits, is free; its phenomenal manifestations are determined. And they are determined, I think, because they are *partial* manifestations, hence fall under the category of causality by reason of the connection of part with part, or of part and whole.

---

[1] Thus we find Descartes asserting that the will "must assent to what I clearly conceive while I so conceive it"; and that consequently perception of understanding should always precede judgment of the will (cf. p. 15 supra).

So, again, in the Voluntarism of M. Bergson. The Vital Impulse is, from its very nature as the ultimate reality from which all is derived, a free force. It may be fanciful to trace an analogy between the determination of Schopenhauer's phenomenal manifestations and the determination admitted by M. Bergson in all acts which do not proceed from the self as a whole, whereas he holds that free action is action that emanates from the whole personality. But is this not a case of freedom *because* it is the whole personality that is involved? As such, it is self-determined. But Schopenhauer admits no such wholeness of personality to be phenomenally manifested, for he always regards the person as a phenomenal manifestation of the will in itself, and, therefore, a *partial* manifestation.

It seems to me, finally, that M. Bergson has left freedom as little force in our daily life as Kant did, and if he does not "conduct it with all due ceremony into the intemporal realm of things-in-themselves[1]," he places it in the depths of a deep-seated ego which is attained rarely by anyone, and never by some.

Practically, we have the consciousness of freedom, but I do not think that any of these philosophers have vindicated more than this. That the Vital Impulse, fundamental will, or whatever designation one gives to ultimate reality voluntaristically conceived, is *free* cannot, I think, be denied from the voluntaristic standpoint. That we, as fragments of the whole, are free in the same ultimate sense, is not, it seems to me, proved by the same arguments.

Freedom as self-determination is, then, we conclude, essential to all forms of voluntarism. Prof. James, however, means much more than this, and condemns the

[1] *D.I.C.* p. 183 (E. Tr. p. 238).

tendency to "soft determinism," by which he seems to have meant "self-determination." In his view the issue between determinists and indeterminists "is a perfectly sharp one which no eulogistic terminology can smear over or wipe out," for "the question relates solely to the existence of possibilities, in the strict sense of the term, as things that may, but need not, be[1]."

He is anxious to assert the reality of '*chance*' as a fact of reality and not as an expression of incomplete knowledge. Slightly softened down into the phrase "possibility of real alternatives," the conception of chance is admitted by the whole 'philosophy of contingency' as represented by Renouvier, Boutroux and Bergson. This is certainly the impression derived from *L'Evolution Créatrice*, although in his discussion of the question of the predictability of human actions, M. Bergson does not so much deny, or admit, the possibility of real alternative courses of action, as point out the futility of asking such a question.

M. Fouillée, on the other hand, is strongly opposed to the admission of contingency into the conception of the universe. Nevertheless, although he denies that such alternative possibilities do exist in *reality*, yet he argues that because we do not *know* the future it is really indetermined *for us*. Hence we can form an ideal and have power to realise it. Our idea, then, is a factor of the future. Further, it is our activity that constitutes the law; not the law that determines our activity. He concludes, then, that the universe is not shut up by its determinism but is capable of indefinite moral progress.

We shall have occasion later to consider how far the

---

[1] *The Dilemma of Determinism*, p. 151.

recognition of will as a real factor necessitates the admission of the complete indetermination of reality.

M. Fouillée differs from other French Voluntarists in his attitude towards intellect; he protests against the separation of intellect from will, regarding the latter as more fundamental, yet as inseparably bound in human consciousness with the intellectual element.

This, it seems to me, is expressed in the title he chooses to denote his philosophy "idées-forces," and in the expression "volonté de conscience," which, in *La Morale des Idées-forces*, he used to sum up the ultimate reality, on the analogy of Nietzsche's "Will to Power," but laying stress, in opposition to all such one-sided theories, on consciousness as a whole, intellect and will combined. It is on this account, that it seems desirable to describe the "philosophie des idées-forces" as intellectualistic voluntarism.

(2) Allied, in some respects, with the trend of thought expressed in M. Fouillée's philosophy is the work of his step-son J. M. Guyau, whose death at the early age of thirty-three prevented the complete development of his philosophy, which seemed to be tending—in spite of his adoption of the theory of "idées-forces"—in the direction of "creative evolution."

The fundamental conception of Guyau's philosophy is the idea of *life*, which, he holds, is the synthesis to unite mind and matter. "We can affirm with certainty," he says, "that life, by the very fact of its development, tends to engender consciousness; and that progress in life ultimately comes to be one with progress in consciousness, in which, what is movement in one aspect, is sensation in another[1]."

[1] *L'Irréligion de l'Avenir* (E. Tr. p. 494).

Life is essentially productivity, force, expansion; it is "activity in one or other of its more or less equivalent forms: moral activity and what may be called metaphysical activity." Hence, "the world is one continuous Becoming." The activity of life is expressed in various forms. Thought is one of its principal forms, because "thought is, so to speak, condensed action and life at its maximum development[1]." It is the highest development of life just because it is concentrated activity and not Aristotle's "pure action" freed from contact with matter. The distinction between will and intelligence must not be made so great that it becomes necessary to bring in feeling to move the will. Thought itself is the commencement of action, and indeed "it may be said that will is but a superior degree of intelligence, and that action is but a superior degree of will[2]."

Guyau thus adopts Fouillée's theory of "Idées-forces," and indeed goes beyond it in declaring that thought and action are "fundamentally identical." It seems, however, that he means by this only that thought tends to be realised in action, or, as Fouillée puts it, "the idea is already itself the consciousness of a movement commenced, of a change in process of being accomplished and which cannot come to an abrupt cessation[3]." It is the "sense of the profound identity that exists between thought and action[4]" that supplies, Guyau thinks, the power of moral obligation, for obligation is not an external force, but an "internal expansion—a need to complete our ideas by converting them into action[2]." The expansion of life is thus the principle and the end of activity; the aim of

---

[1] *Sketch of Morality*, p. 76.   [2] *Ibid.* p. 93.
[3] *Evol. des I.-f.* p. lxix.   [4] *Sketch of Morality*, p. 211.

conscious action is the same as the cause of unconscious action, and this cause is life itself, for "life unfolds and expresses itself in activity because it is life[1]." Power to act, Guyau holds, is itself an obligation;—" I can, therefore I must"; the principle of morality becomes "life the most intensive and the most extensive possible."

This conception of life, as including in its intensity a principle of expansion, Guyau made the common foundation of his theory of art, morals and religion.

The resemblances between Guyau's principle of life and Nietzsche's "Will to Power" are as obvious as they are striking. But while for Nietzsche, life is incessant and painful strife, for Guyau it is joyful activity that requires no justification and no goal other than its own continuance. So, too, for Bergson the Vital-Impulse is an endless creative activity which carries its justification in itself. In its completed development the philosophy of Guyau would, I think, have approached more nearly to the philosophy of creative evolution than to Fouillée's "idées-forces." Not only does Guyau resemble Bergson in the conception of life as the fundamental reality which in itself is an expansive force, and in the conception of time, which indeed seems to be bound up with the former, but he tends towards an alogical theory of reality that Fouillée would be forced to reject.

It is interesting to find that Guyau recognised a psychological, heterogeneous time, distinct from the mathematical time of the geometrician and astronomer, which he explicitly declared to be derived from representing time by space. It is in this heterogeneous time that the spiritual life "s'écoule." It is true that Bergson has expressed the

[1] *Sketch of Morality*, p. 77.

theory with much greater force and clearness, and has explicitly connected "duration" with the "vital impulse," hence has made a considerable advance on Guyau's conception. Nevertheless, the resemblance extends, in some points, even to matters of detail. Whether or not, therefore, M. Bergson owes anything directly to the influence of Guyau it may be difficult to decide, but there is a close affinity between them, closer, it seems to me, than between Guyau and Fouillée, for, although the former adopted the theory of "idées-forces," he parted company with Fouillée in affirming that the sense of life suffices for philosophy, and in emphasising its alogical aspect. Theory of knowledge, Guyau says, must be subordinated to theory of life; knowledge and its laws are derived from the needs and laws of life. "To sum up," he says, "it is *action* and the power of life which alone can solve—if not entirely, at least partially—those problems to which abstract thought gives rise[1]."

The view that action can cut the knot of problems raised by abstract thought seems to me open to many objections. It is, however, one that is becoming increasingly prominent, and has been very clearly expressed by M. Séailles. To separate thought and action is, M. Séailles insists, to destroy the unity of life. We know only in proportion as we act with sincerity and moral earnestness. There is no opposition between speculative and practical activity for " the analysis which thus opposes thought and will, man who knows and man who acts, is an artificial analysis which destroys the unity of life. He who separates action from thought condemns himself to a semi-scepticism the uncertainties of which cannot fail to appear

[1] *Sketch of Morality*, p. 214.

in his conduct[1]." Thus he asserts "Every action is affirmation."

This does not appear to me to be tenable. While it is obvious that thought and action cannot be opposed, in so far as we cannot think one thing and do another without glaring inconsistency, in no clear sense can it be said that "one can doubt what one *says*, but not what one *does*," meaning thereby, that action gives truth while thought, as Séailles says, may be uncertain because it carries with it no affirmation of existence. There is, of course, a certain definiteness in action, in so far as when one acts one perforce does one thing to the exclusion of any other; but, similarly, in so far as one thinks a thing, it is thought to the exclusion of the opposite, i.e. it involves an affirmation that is no less definite. One may think one thing and do another; both are "affirmations" in one sense; yet neither is more definite than the other, i.e. less untrustworthy, less obviously true apart from further criterion. The transference of the word "affirmation" from the sphere of thought to that of action, and the consequent bringing in of action to solve the problems raised by intellect, leads only to confusion. It is true that action and thought, intellect and will cannot be opposed, that reasoning in concrete life is never isolated from feeling and will. But this does not imply that the intellectual aspect of a given situation cannot be considered in abstraction from the other elements in the concrete whole.

This confusion lies at the root of the pragmatist position and it is found in Guyau and M. Séailles.

[1] *Les Affirmations de la Conscience Moderne*, p. 146.

III. CONCLUSION

I.

1. WE may sum up French Voluntarism as developing along three lines:

(A) The main line, direct from Maine de Biran, including Ravaisson, Boutroux, Bergson, Le Roy and Wilbois, we have denominated Spiritualistic Activism by reason of its adoption of the standpoint of personal experience as fundamental and its insistence upon the predominantly active character of that experience. In its later development it tends in the direction of mysticism, and is properly an "Intuitionism" akin to the German Romantic philosophy both of Schelling and Schopenhauer. While anti-intellectualistic it is also distinctly anti-pragmatic. Closely allied is the "philosophy of action" of MM. Blondel and Laberthonnière.

(B) A second line is that of Neo-Criticism as represented by Renouvier and his School. This is a moralism derived mainly from Kant's practical philosophy; it has some affinities with Pragmatism, but there are essential differences.

(C) Thirdly, there is the "philosophie des idées-forces," which differs on the one hand from the Intuitionism of Bergson, and on the other from the Moralism of Renouvier; it neither disparages intellect as M. Bergson does by regarding it as disqualified for the service of truth, nor does it look to moral affirmations as Renouvier does, to fill up the gaps that intellect fails to cross; it may perhaps be most correctly described as an " Intellectualistic Voluntarism."

Voluntarists, then, differ as to what should be substituted for intellect as the faculty by which truth is to be attained. The pragmatist substitutes will and desire and subordinates truth to interest ; the Bergsonian intuitionist professes to have found an additional faculty, intuition, which is the philosophic faculty *par excellence* because it alone is competent to attain truth, for it alone is able to " transcend the human condition " which, M. Bergson says, it must be the aim of philosophy to do[1]. In one of his striking similes M. Bergson says that science — the elaborated knowledge of ordinary life — has thrown a bridge across the river, and metaphysics has dug a tunnel beneath it, but both alike have left the river untouched. It is the peculiar work of philosophy to plunge into the river of life which is perpetual movement, unrestrained freedom, change itself.

2. Reality as conceived by M. Bergson is, we have seen, incessant movement, the continuous elaboration of the absolutely new. Novelty, change, chance, these are the characteristics of reality as free creative activity. It

[1] "In the living mobility of things the understanding is bent on marking real or possible stations, it notes departures and arrivals ; for this is all that concerns the thought of man in so far as it is simply human. It is more than human to grasp what is happening in the interval. But philosophy can only be an effort to transcend the human condition." (*R.M.M.* 1903, p. 30, E. Tr. p. 65.)

has been pointed out that the admission of radical contingency is characteristic of French Voluntarism both in
the later development of Spiritualistic Activism in the
philosophies of Boutroux and Bergson, and in the philosophy
of Renouvier, the outcome of whose " Neo-Criticism " was
the assertion of real possibilities, summed up by James
as belief "in absolute novelties, unmediated beginnings,
gifts, chance, freedom and acts of faith[1]."

Freedom of the self is fundamental with de Biran, and
the freedom of self-determination is, I have contended,
admitted in the "rectified determinism " of M. Fouillée.
A distinction must, then, be drawn between the freedom
of self-determination which is essential to all forms of
voluntarism and that freedom of utter indetermination
which James proclaimed as chance and which has been
endorsed by the philosophy of contingency and creative
evolution.

Two questions are forced upon us. First, does the
recognition of will as a real factor, hence of the reality
of personal activity, involve complete indetermination of
reality, that is, the admission of chance ? Secondly, is
intellectual activity essentially uncreative and determined?
The whole point of the discussion here lies in the force we
attribute to the terms involved, and it will be well
to consider another question first. In what does creative
activity consist ?

The essence of creative activity is not, it seems to me,
the production of the absolutely new and unforeseeable by

---

[1] *Some Problems of Philosophy*, p. 164. It may be noted that James
professed to have worked out his conception of free will as chance under
the influence of Renouvier (see *loc. cit.* (note) and *Will to Believe*,
p. 143).

which is meant that the production is essentially something that could not be foreseen because it transcends logical formulation, being a creation *ex nihilo*. M. Bergson cites the case of a painter whom we see before his canvas with the colours ready and the model posed, and he asks whether, possessing the elements of the problem, we can foresee the picture that is to be painted. He replies that we cannot for " the concrete solution brings with it that unforeseeable nothing which is the whole of a work of art[1]." In this unaccountability, due to pure novelty, lies, for M. Bergson, the essence of artistic creation which is one with the creative activity of life.

But a work of art, because it is creative, is not pure novelty, a complete breaking away from all conditions ; so far from being non-rational, it is the supremely rational and could be logically formulated, hence foreseeable, were we at a sufficiently high level of reason.

There lies, I think, at the root of M. Bergson's conception of creative activity, a conception of art as irresponsible, incalculable " freedom " that escapes the grasp of intellect, which he has already prejudged as the faculty of binding the same to the same. But if it be granted that creation in art is essentially an ordered activity that transcends not logic, nor intellect as such, but only our powers of logical formulation, then we can admit that freedom is not chance but self-determination in a deeper sense than any non-rational voluntaristic conception can give us. It is deeper because it is not an arbitrary freedom but logical and rational proceeding from the whole personality. That such is the real significance of freedom M. Bergson has himself admitted when he said, " it is from

[1] *Ev. Cr.* p. 368 (E. Tr. p. 360).

the whole soul, in fact that the free decision springs[1] ";
where there is wholeness of personality there is a freedom.
It is true that M. Bergson himself is apt to forget this,
and that his distinction between the two selves finally
leads him to lose sight of personality and to banish
freedom much as Kant had done[2]. It is his unduly
narrow view of intellect that is responsible for this result.

In opposition to M. Bergson, then, we find that true
freedom is realised in the creative activity of intellect
proceeding logically and that such creation is not
essentially incalculable. Freedom is not therefore contingency.

To the second question raised above we reply, then,
that intellectual activity is truly creative and finds its
highest expression in art, interpreted in its widest sense.
Further, in this is found, I think, the answer to the first
question. The activity of will is not necessarily a blind
activity; in its highest manifestations it is rational activity.
The self as a whole is a real factor in the universe but it is
continuous with it; it is creative, but just because creative
activity does not mean creation *ex abrupto,* so will as a
real factor does not involve complete indetermination of
reality. The completion of will is found not in the
discontinuity of arbitrary choice and contingency, but in
the fulfilment of the principle of personality, the true
originality.

NOTE.—When we consider the conception of contingency in French
Voluntarism, we see how different is the meaning of Dr Ward when he
admits that his philosophy "lets contingency into the very heart of
things," for he adds, " the contingency is not that of chance but that of
freedom," and he proceeds to explain this as rational necessity, the
freedom of purposive activity (see *Naturalism and Agnosticism,* Vol. II.

[1] *D.I.C.* p. 128.   [2] See supra, p. 148.

pp. 280—1 ; 2nd Ed.). There is, I think, here an indication of the view
of freedom as founded on a true conception of personality which I have
been endeavouring to suggest; but Dr Ward seems anxious to retain
"contingency" as opposed to "logical determination," whereas it is this
latter conception which appears to me to be compatible with freedom as
creative activity and essential to a true conception of personality. It is
the recognition of freedom within logical determination that is needed,
I think, before it would be possible to solve the difficulty Dr Ward points
out of reconciling " our wills are ours " with the supremacy of God or
the Absolute. From M. Bergson's point of view it remains, I think,
insoluble, and would appear insurmountable so long as freedom is taken
to exclude logical determination.

3. The view of the Bergsonian intuitionist that creative
activity is essentially alogical, hence his failure to obtain a
true conception of personality and freedom, is the outcome
of the restricted function he assigns to intellect and the
consequent denial of any intellectual element in art.

It has already been pointed out that M. Bergson
assumes that intellect is "intended to secure the perfect
fitting of our body to its environment, to represent the
relations of external things among themselves, and in
short, to think matter[1]." He conceives on the one hand
an intelligence that is a mere form, on the other an
activity that is pure heterogeneity. To these correspond
two selves; one a spatialised self adapted to action ; the
other an enduring self that lives the real. These are
opposed as pure homogeneity to pure heterogeneity, as
quantity to quality, as immobility to continuous movement.
This dualism corresponds to the dualism of the real as
matter and life, or spirit. We have observed above that
M. Bergson at first regards the distinction between them
as one of degree only; matter is a limit at one extreme,
spirit is a limit at the other extreme. When, however, he

[1] *Ev. Cr.* p. i.

comes to derive them from the same impulse of the "vital impulse," he regards them as diverse and opposed. Consequently there are two opposed ways of knowing: by intellect we know matter, by intuition we know spirit by insertion within the ascending life current. At times M. Bergson seems anxious to insist that *both* forms of knowing give us knowledge of absolute reality ; he protests that "it is reality in itself, absolute reality, which the mathematical and physical sciences tend to reveal to us[1]," but they fail to do so completely owing to the necessity of posing the problems one after another !

But in spite of this protest, M. Bergson frequently speaks as though intellect were incapable of giving any knowledge of absolute reality, for the knowledge that it gives is always relative to action, and the needs of action, M. Bergson continually insists, *distort* our apprehension of reality. Intellect is the faculty that has been evolved to subserve the needs of action and adapt us to our material environment. In a noteworthy passage M. Bergson says, "If it (intellect) were intended for pure theory, it is within movement that it would place itself, for movement is undoubtedly reality itself," but he adds, "Intelligence, in its natural state, aims at a practically useful end[2]," and the philosopher errs when he transfers to the domain of speculation "a method of thought which is made for action."

The opposition between such a view and Pragmatism is marked. While M. Bergson condemns the intellect because it *is* pragmatic, the pragmatist condemns any view of the structure of intellect that makes it *not* pragmatic, and repudiates the "pure intellect" of the intellectualist because it takes no consideration of utility.

[1] *B.S.F.Ph.* 1903, p. 21.   [2] *Ev. Cr.* p. 168.

For M. Bergson obviously "utility" is not the way to truth; indeed, it seems rather to be synonymous with error, for, in a passage already cited, he remarks that just *because* the division of reality is effected under the influence of our needs it does not follow the real structure of things[1].

But surely, we may ask, is it not odd that if our intellect distort matter it should be useful and adapt us to it ? We are living, M. Bergson seems to say, in a world built up by intellect in the interests of action but which does not resemble "reality" for, the better to subserve our needs, "reality" has been deformed. This is an extreme of pessimistic scepticism that may well seem to justify a plunge into Pragmatism by way of reaction ! "If this be the case," it may be said, "then let us call this ' distorted world ' the reality, and bother not at all about that *other* reality that is so unsuited to us ! "

I think that the reply Bergson might make is that a radical distinction must be made between two *kinds* of life : the lower is adapted to the " distorted reality," whereas "reality itself" is adapted only to the higher spiritual life, and that these are attainable by intellect and intuition respectively.

In this case three questions call for consideration ; (*a*) Is not instinct, of which we may take it, intuition is a more developed form, more radically bound to action than intellect, hence, is it not more useful ? (*b*) What is the relation of utility and truth, and why must we reject alike the pragmatist's identification of them and Bergson's complete divorce ? (*c*) Can such a radical distinction between the lower and the higher " life " be made, for does it not involve an untenable dualism of the self ?

[1] *M. et M.* p. 202 and p. 73 supra.

(*a*) It is not necessary to elaborate instances to show that instinct is of immense use in adapting the animal to his environment, and that it appears to have been evolved for this purpose. If it were knowledge at all it would certainly be *useful* knowledge, and useful for purely animal ends. It is true that Bergson says that instinct fails because it is turned exclusively to action, but he asserts that if it were diverted to knowledge and became conscious, it would be knowledge of the real that it would give us. But would this knowledge cease to be useful? If not, would it not be true? The assumption, further, that "our needs" are necessarily corporeal needs, needs of action in its lowest sense, is surely unjustifiable. To assume this is to degrade man to the brute level, to deny him any aspirations other than those of the lower animals which may possibly be sufficiently provided for by a knowledge of matter that is adequate to adapt them to their environment. But man seeks other ends than the preservation of his body. To reply that intuition will supply these needs is to beg the question for it has not yet been proved that the function of the intellect is restricted to the needs of bodily activity, and the *onus probandi* lies with those who deny that these higher demands are not the product of man's rational nature and capable of satisfaction by means of it. The appeal to a transformed instinct here is as unnecessary as it is futile.

(*b*) In the consideration of the relation between truth and utility M. Bergson and his disciples are at the opposite pole from Pragmatism. We have seen that M. Wilbois, when discussing non-Euclidean geometries, made a distinction in favour of Euclidean space on the ground that it is more "commode" and is suggested by our experience, while he refused to admit that it is more *true* than, for example, Lowatchewski's[1]. I have pointed out that this position is contradictory and that in so far as Euclidean space is suggested by our experience and conformable to it, it would seem to correspond to reality in a way that other "spaces" do not, and should for that reason be called true.

The use Dr Schiller makes of non-Euclidean geometries is to illustrate his thesis that axioms are postulates and that the axiom of parallels was postulated by Euclid because he wanted it, and any other of the contradictory postulates would have given just as useful results if we had been differently constituted. Hence he concludes that Euclidean space, spherical, and pseudo-spherical space are all three equally valid[2], but Euclidean space is more useful and "is true because it works and in so far as it works[3]." That is, Dr Schiller equates the useful with the true ; M. Wilbois equates the useful with the not-true.

Both start from the same assumption, which seems to me untenable, viz. there are many geometries any one of which is applicable to space as we know it. Both agree that Euclidean space is most convenient because it fits our needs and habits best, as it were by chance. They differ only in their conclusions : Dr Schiller argues that since Euclidean space is most useful and works it is true[4] ;

[1] p. 72 supra.

[2] I regret that in the paper read before the Aristotelian Society in which these paragraphs appeared, Dr Schiller's view of space was inadvertently misrepresented, and the necessary correction of "valid" for "real" was not made in the published volumes of the Society's proceedings.

[3] *Personal Idealism*, p. 114.

[4] See *Personal Idealism*, p. 114. "Our assumption, then, of geometrical space is true because it works and in so far as it works." It is true that Dr Schiller goes on to ask, "But does it work?" and he

the "New Philosopher" argues that since Euclidean space is most useful it must be admitted that it is suggested by our experience, but because it is useful it cannot be *true* for our needs distort reality, and because the other geometries are conceivably useful they cannot be true, therefore *none are true*.

I hold that both conclusions are wrong. First I have disputed the assumption that non-Euclidean geometries are equally applicable to our space. Hence the pragmatist appears to me right in saying Euclidean space is true, but he is wrong in identifying this truth with its usefulness; the "New Philosopher" appears to me to be quite wrong when he argues that utility necessarily disqualifies for truth.

Similar arguments apply to the general contention that use distorts reality. In summing up then the relation of utility and truth I should argue that what is true is useful in the widest sense, i.e. useful theoretically and practically; but I should also contend that what is useful is not necessarily true because reality is not perfectly harmonious. In any case it would be impossible to identify truth with utility because it is but a consequence of truth that it is useful. The pragmatist first identifies truth with its consequences, then selects one of these, viz. utility, and substitutes one for the other. But the utility depends on the truth and not *vice versa*. Hence the equation of the useful and the true is not justifiable; still less so, perhaps, is its identification with error.

concludes that "Euclidian geometry is fully competent to do the work we demand of our geometrical construction," whilst pointing out that "that does not make it more real than its rivals." Nevertheless, this does not seem to me to alter the force of his statement that *in so far as* Euclidean geometry *works* it is *true*.

(c) The distinction that M. Bergson makes between the lower life of intellect and the higher life of intuition is equivalent to the distinction between the fundamental and the superficial self and corresponds to the opposed movements within the "vital impulse" that give us spirit and matter. In *L'Evolution Créatrice* the theory of the self elaborated in the *Essai* is applied to reality as a whole. This splitting of the self into two appears an extreme device to ensure human freedom but it does so only by establishing within the self a dualism comparable to that of mind and matter—a comparison that is further borne out by Bergson's study of their relation. In spite, therefore, of M. Bergson's protest, noted above[1], that the self must not be regarded as "split up," it must be admitted that the distinction established is radical and constitutes an irreconcilable conflict between the two selves.

4. There is, then, on one side a spatialised self adapted to know "matter in the pure state" by means of intellect, and on the other, a deep-seated self that by means of intuition is inserted within the current of life, or duration, hence *knows* ultimate reality. It has already been pointed out that M. Bergson is apparently inconsistent in his view as to the nature of the knowledge given us by intellect. It may be that the reason of this inconsistency is that M. Bergson regards duration as ultimately real in a sense in which matter is not, so that it would be possible to regard knowledge of the former as knowledge, in a deeper sense, of reality. But if this be the explanation, it must nevertheless be acknowledged that numerous passages could be cited to support the view that they are regarded

---

[1] p. 9 supra.

as equally significant knowledge of "halves of the real[1]."

There are thus two ways of knowing, and while science, knowledge of material reality, is the work of intellect, philosophy, knowledge of "living reality," is the work of intuition. It is necessary, therefore, to estimate the value of intuition.

5. Among the various shades of meaning that have been attributed to the term "intuition" there are two so well marked that it is advisable to consider them before dealing with intuition as a philosophical method. In its ordinary use in everyday life intuition means sympathetic insight, an apprehension that does not lend itself to logical formulation. In philosophy intuition is frequently used to denote sense-perception, as in translation of Kant's term "Anschauung."

There is a common element in these two meanings, in that both imply immediate apprehension, hence closeness of contact with the object intuited. It is this element that is emphasised in M. Bergson's use of the term "intuition" to suggest an immediate apprehension akin to sense-perception in which—to use the words of Locke— "the mind is at no pains of proving or examining, but perceives the truth, as the eye does light, only by being directed towards it[2]."

Such a direct contact with or "perception" of the real is the aim of M. Bergson's Intuitionism, and in his Oxford lectures he connects it with the work of Kant, pointing out that Kant recognised the supreme need for intuition—

---

[1] See *Ev. Cr.* p. 370, where there is a mingling of the two points of view, in which Bergson's anti-pragmatism is obvious.

[2] Essay IV. ii. sect. 1.

or "vision"—and that it was his inability to find it that led him to his negative conclusion. "Only," he says, "a higher intuition (which Kant calls an '*intellectual*' intuition), that is to say a *perception* of metaphysical reality, would give to metaphysical science the means of being constituted. The clearest result of the Kantian *Critique* is thus to demonstrate that one can penetrate into the beyond only by a vision, and that a doctrine has value, in this sphere, only in so far as it contains perception[1]."

Thus the true method of attaining philosophical truth is to abandon discursive reasoning, or dialectic, which "leads us to opposed philosophies[2]," and to trust ourselves to an effort of intuition.

The reference to Kant is worthy of note. M. Bergson's intuition is no less an appeal from knowledge to something other than knowledge than is Kant's appeal to noumenal knowledge. He is faced by an even greater difficulty of saying anything about the intuition owing to his radical separation of intuition from conception, since concepts "*negate* the real" by manipulating it in the interests of action. But intuition is essentially disinterested ; it is an attempt to "see for the sake of seeing."

Such disinterestedness of view is found in its highest and purest form only in art. To art then we must turn if we would attain a knowledge of reality free from admixture of utilitarian elements. We penetrate the nature of reality only in so far as we attain the artistic standpoint. Hence to illustrate the application of their philosophical method MM. Bergson and Le Roy make frequent appeals to art, generally pictorial art. Throughout, the analogy

[1] *P.C.* p. 15. Cf. *R.M.M.* 1911, juillet, p. xviii.
[2] *P.C.* p. 14.

of artistic intuition is apparent; it becomes in·fact more than an analogy.

M. Bergson's view of the relation of Art to Reality is very clearly brought out in his essay on the significance of the comic—*Le Rire.* What, he asks, is the purpose of art?

"If reality could come into direct contact with sense and consciousness, could we enter into immediate communion with things and with ourselves, I believe that art would be useless, or rather we should all be artists, for then our soul would continually vibrate in perfect accord with nature. Deep in our souls we should hear the strains of our inner life's unbroken melody. All this is around us and within us, and yet no whit of it do we distinctly perceive. Between nature and ourselves, nay, between ourselves and our own consciousness, a veil is interposed; a veil that is dense and opaque for the common herd, thin, almost transparent, for the artist and the poet. What fairy wove the veil? Was it done in malice or in friendliness? We had to live, and life demands that we grasp things in their relations to our own needs. Life is action. Life implies the acceptance only of the *utilitarian* side of things in order to respond to them by appropriate reaction....My senses and my consciousness, give me no more than a practical simplification of reality....The *individuality* of things or of beings escapes us, unless it is materially to our advantage to perceive it[1]."

Nevertheless, the veil drawn by the needs of life over the reality of things can, M. Bergson thinks, be pierced,

"From time to time, however, in a fit of absentmindedness, nature raises up souls that are more detached from life."

This detachment is not, however, the reasoned, systematic detachment that is "the result of reflection and philosophy," but the detachment of the artist, who sees only for the sake of seeing; yet

"were this detachment complete, did the soul no longer cleave to

[1] *Le Rire,* pp. 153 *seq.* (E. Tr. pp. 150 *seq.*).

action by any of its perceptions, it would be the soul of an artist such as the world has never yet seen. It would excel alike in every art at the same time; or rather it would fuse them all into one. It would perceive all things in their native purity : the forms, colours, sounds of the physical world as well as the subtlest movements of the inner life[1]."

Thus would be realised the highest ambition of art, for

"art has no other object than to brush aside the utilitarian symbols, the conventional and socially accepted generalities, in short, everything that veils reality from us, in order to bring us face to face with reality itself[2]."

The standpoint of the philosopher and the artist is the same, or, rather the artist is the true philosopher. To attempt to translate the living reality in terms of explicit thought is to seek to express the inexpressible. Only immediate intuition—disinterested intuition such as the artist's—is adequate to grasp the real. The standpoint adopted is that of the artist at work, not of the spectator contemplating a work of art, nor of the artist himself when he reviews his own work. The emphasis lies on his creative activity in which he and his object are one, and he may be said to *know* his object only because he *is* it. The importance of this will be seen later in estimating the value of this theory for the attainment of Truth. That such an identity of the knower and the known is meant can be the only interpretation of M. Bergson's description of the true philosophical method as one in which one "enters into a thing" and "coincides with it." It is no less clearly stated by M. Le Roy—

"Images are not portraits nor symbols...of I know not what external beings. They are not simple states of the self without

[1] *Le Rire*, p. 158 (E. Tr. p. 154).   [2] *Ibid.* p. 161 (E. Tr. p. 157).

absolute consistency, a species of unreal phantoms. No, they ought to be called neither objective nor subjective, being prior to the process of abstraction which gives a meaning to these adjectives. We ourselves make at first part of the images and are them all successively[1]."

Truth is living reality and is known only by living it, by the immediate seizing of intuition. It is essentially inexpressible, hence can only be indicated by the help of metaphors, of which both M. Bergson and M. Le Roy make abundant use.

Thus it is not by chance that M. Bergson expresses himself by metaphor piled on metaphor. He is forced by the necessity of his method to suggest by metaphor what escapes the limits of clear thought. His metaphors are not mere superfluous adornment, tricks of oratory, but a vital part of his philosophy. It is, therefore, as has been frequently pointed out, futile either to argue with M. Bergson or to seek arguments that support his position. He uses no argument; he states his views with eloquence and supports them with metaphors, but he offers no loophole for discussion. The philosophy of creative evolution is indemonstrable, and he does not seek to demonstrate it. Either one will accept it and share in the intuition, or one will not. In either case, there is an end of the matter.

The unsatisfactoriness of this resort to immediate intuition as the basis of a philosophy is clearly brought out, in another connection, by Mr Joachim who criticises it on the ground that an "immediate intuition" is "a belief which the believer cannot justify, or at any rate has not yet justified, by rational grounds[2]."

To this MM. Bergson and Le Roy would undoubtedly

[1] *R.M.M.* 1901, p. 422. [2] *Nature of Truth*, p. 55.

reply that to attempt so to justify intuition by rational grounds would be to degrade it and detract from its original purity. But, as Mr Joachim also points out, it is only in so far as experience is raised to the level of mediate thought that the question of truth can arise. "It is," he says, "in the attempt to mediate our 'immediate experiences' that their truth or falsity is revealed; and except in so far as that attempt is made, and in being made succeeds or fails, they possess for us neither truth nor falsity[1]."

The resort to intuition in metaphysics gives rise to serious difficulties. It involves an extreme individualism. Each individual has his own intuition which cannot be expressed nor defended; there can be only reiteration without argument. Even if the intuition were expressible, it could not be refuted, for, since the appeal *is* to immediate intuition, there is no criterion that may decide between rival intuitions. It lays itself open, therefore, to many of the objections that have been offered against the "moral sense." In each case, "orthodoxy is my opinion, heterodoxy is other people's opinions"!

We are forced, then, on this theory to conclude that philosophy has no greater universality than art. This is a position which some at least of these philosophers are willing to take up. M. Laberthonnière, for instance, insists that philosophy is an art, and, moreover, an art in which all must participate since all must live, and living implies a metaphysic consciously or unconsciously accepted. There seems, however, to be some confusion here. Just as there is a science of Aesthetics, so there is a science of "living" (in M. Laberthonnière's sense of the term "living"), and

[1] *Ibid.* p. 57.

this science is philosophy. It is not of course a positive science nor a normative science, but a system of knowledge which claims universality just as much as the exact sciences do, but with no more pretension to finality. To argue that, because a man's life involves a whole metaphysic, that, *therefore*, metaphysics is the *art* of living, seems to me to be analogous to arguing that because bodily movements are in conformity with, and therefore involve the laws of, positive science, that, *therefore*, such science is the *art* of bodily movement. ˙ The object of philosophy is the attainment and communication of knowledge of Reality. In so far as the line between science and art is clearly drawn, philosophy is a science and not an art. We shall never learn philosophy by living it, any more than we shall know what justice is only by doing just actions.

M. Bergson is led to adopt the standpoint of art because he holds that to know a thing as it is, one must *be* it. The distinction between subject and object, the antithesis between the act of knowing and the thing known, is thus to be abolished in the interests of knowledge itself.

But, as Lotze has pointed out, such an antithesis is involved in the very meaning of knowledge, which "will never *be* the thing itself but only an aggregate of ideas *about* the thing." Thus "he who demands a knowledge which should be more than a perfectly connected and consistent system of ideas about the thing, a knowledge which should actually exhaust the thing itself, is no longer asking for knowledge at all, but for something entirely unintelligible[1]."

MM. Bergson and Le Roy might perhaps reply that it is " unintelligible " because above intellect and deeper than

[1] *Logic* (E. Tr.), Bk. III. Ch. I. Sect. 308.

knowledge. Indeed, their constant use of such expressions as "union" and "communion" with the real would seem to involve a reference to something "deeper" than knowledge. In this case the conception of knowledge would be meaningless, and the question of truth and falsity would cease to exist[1].

A theory of knowledge that makes such intuition the supreme philosophical method is confronted with two dangers—either that of scepticism, or of vagueness so extreme as to be compatible with any metaphysical theory by affording no criterion that can determine which is true, and hence leads back again to scepticism for "everything is possible, and everybody is right"!

Intuition is, by definition, individual and incommunicable. When, therefore, we have dived down into the living duration that is the object of the Bergsonian intuition, we cannot state the result of our experience. It may be that we are not—as M. Bergson assures us we are not—shut up to the contemplation of ourself, but are put into "contact with a whole continuity of durations[2]"; but we are unable to state the fact or convince anyone else of the contact.

Thus it would appear that this intuition is essentially akin to that religious intuition which finds expression in an exclamation such as F. W. H. Myers', "O could I tell,

[1] There seems to be an indication of this position in the conclusion reached by Dr McTaggart in his attempt to determine the nature of the Absolute. There is, he thinks, "a possibility of finding, above all knowledge and volition, one all-embracing unity, which is only not true, only not good, because all truth and all goodness are but distorted shadows of its absolute perfection, "das Unbegreifliche, weil es der Begriff selbst ist." Here admittedly neither knowledge nor truth exists.

[2] *R.M.M.* 1903, p. 25.

ye surely would believe it!" But the vision cannot be told. From the philosophical point of view the difficulty is that a metaphysic exists for the purpose of expressing the "vision" and a theory of knowledge as a means thereto.

That such is the outcome of this intuitionism would appear to be recognised by M. Bergson in that he holds that all philosophical systems are at bottom essentially agreed, that is, in so far as they are derived by means of intuition; but they differ in the course of development which depends upon the conceptual analysis of the original intuition. All systems are, therefore, true in so far as "vivified by intuition," inadequate and false in their development by dialectic. But, M. Bergson says "dialectic is necessary to put intuition to the proof, necessary also in order that intuition should break itself up into concepts and so be propagated to other men; but often it only develops the result of that intuition which transcends it" but, "intuition, if it could be prolonged beyond a few instants, would ensure not only the agreement of the philosopher with his own thought, but also all philosophers with each other[1]."

But the theory of intuition itself affords, however, no suggestion as to how the intuition may be prolonged, nor what criterion may decide the differences which arise when the original and single intuition is expressed, as it necessarily must be, by concepts. It is, indeed, a self-defeating process; the dialectic that is to "put intuition to the proof" is said to proceed in the contrary direction and "the same effort by which ideas are connected with ideas, causes the intuition which the ideas were storing

[1] *Ev. Cr.* p. 259 (E. Tr. p. 252).

up to vanish[1]." It would seem impossible then that the original intuition can be broken up into concepts and communicated to us. The part assigned to dialectic is, therefore, contradictory, and hence it is not shown that the intuition is capable of enlargement into the construction of a metaphysic.

The claim, therefore, that M. Bergson makes[2], to have brought what Kant excluded back into the realm of knowledge, fails for it is the knowledge given by intuition of which Bergson speaks. But this we have seen lacks all the essential marks of knowledge and remains inarticulate.

The conclusion is forced upon us that the result of the Bergsonian Intuitionism is scepticism. On the one hand intellect provides only knowledge that is practically necessary but theoretically invalid; on the other, intuition takes us to the heart of reality but can give us no information about it. Both would give absolute knowledge, intellect of matter, intuition of life, if the movement of reality were completed; but it is not, and it remains impossible for us to transcend the human point of view. This, however, is just what the Bergsonian philosophy requires.

6. The present situation in philosophy was summed up by James in the antithesis "Bradley or Bergson[3]"? Yet, as we have seen, there are differences separating James from Bergson no less fundamental than those which divide the latter from Bradley. Nor do I think that the antithesis thus sharply stated represents accurately the present position. Bradley, James and Bergson alike decry

[1] *Ibid.*
[2] See *B.S.F.Ph.* June 1901, p. 64 and cf. *P.C.* pp. 14—17.
[3] *Journal of Philosophy*, 1910 (Jan.).

knowledge by concepts. James desires "a fuller knowledge in which perception and conception mix their
lights[1]." (This seems to admit that concepts don't
"*negate* the inwardness of reality" or "distort the real,"
but are merely inadequate to the whole reality—a very
different thing.) Bradley fails to find any substitute but
keeps fast to his position that *intellect* must be the faculty
of philosophy, and he resolutely excludes "unmediated
feeling."

Bergson alone claims to have found a deeper kind of
knowing faculty, viz. intuition. It might seem at first
sight that this is the mixture of perception and conception
that James desiderates, and evidently so James takes it.
But this is not so. Concepts, says Bergson, as reported
by James, "*negate* the real, we must then 'drop concepts'";
perception, Bergson is never weary of pointing out, distorts
the real to bring it into accordance with our practical
needs. Both then must be transcended and radically
transformed; we must regress, transcend the human condition and "dive" into the real. But, as has been pointed
out, when this is done we are rendered speechless, for
language is an instrument for adaptation to society and
hence is distortion of the flowing reality. We can attain
a vision, but only a vision that is fleeting, incommunicable,
unsecure. Here "clear ideas" are anathema; the inexpressible is the end sought and the antinomies of
intellect are lost in silence.

The result, then, is well summed up in the sentence
from Plotinus, prefixed, with M. Bergson's permission, by
the translator to *Time and Free Will*—"If a man were to
inquire of Nature the reason of her creative activity, and

---

[1] *loc. cit.*

if she were willing to give ear and answer she would say—
'Ask me not, but understand in silence, even as I am
silent and am not wont to speak.'"

Thus also says Maeterlinck, "Attendons en silence;
peut-être allons-nous percevoir avant peu 'le murmure des
dieux.'"

The question arises—Is this a satisfactory position for
philosophy? If so, it would scarcely seem to require even
the moderate compass of M. Bergson's writings, for the
true philosopher will be the silent mystic, if not the new
born babe!

What then is the comparative value of "clear ideas"
and "mysticism"? Here a distinction must be made
between religion and philosophy. From the point of view
of religion it is not denied that the mystical element may
be of enormous value, and something might possibly be
said for the view that "mysteries" awake awe and
reverence, and hence have a value in religion which might
be lost were the "mysteries" dispelled. But is this a final
ideal? Is it really true that mystery *as such* has beneficial
value? I do not think that this can be maintained. The
value of mystery in religion lies surely in the fact that it
indicates a reality that is beyond our present grasp, a
"presence deeper than knowledge" because our limited
faculties are incompetent to attain it. It is an impetus,
then, to rise above the limitations of our daily life in the
certainty of a wholly satisfying reality that we may attain
in brief vision. But it remains fleeting, rare and incommunicable, just because it transcends our grasp as rational
beings. It is the work of philosophy, it seems to me, to
render the vision stable, persistent and communicable—
that is, to endow it with the qualities of knowledge. In

so doing the vision is not lost; it is heightened and intensified by being rendered clear. The claim of mysticism is, after all, to possess a deeper source of *knowledge*, and it is the work of philosophy to make this truly "knowledge" by bringing it into the sphere of Reason in the widest sense of the term.

II.

7. Throughout this discussion I have assumed that Pragmatism identifies the true and the useful, that is, that its dictum "all truths work" (i.e. are useful) can be converted *simpliciter* into "all that works is true."

Dr Schiller[1], however, on more than one occasion has protested against this assumption. His latest and most explicit rejection of the—to use his own phrase—"grotesque conversion" was made in his paper on *Error* now published in the *Proceedings of the Aristotelian Society*[2]." Nevertheless it must be admitted that this conversion is repeatedly made by James, and is, at least, assumed by all pragmatists, including Dr Schiller himself, for it is essential to the pragmatist position.

In *Pragmatism* (in Lecture VI, dealing with the "notion of truth") James says, "it is useful because it is true" and "it is true because it is useful" "mean exactly the same thing, namely that here is an idea that gets fulfilled and can be verified. True is the name for whatever idea starts the verification process, useful is the name for its completed function in experience[3]." It is true that a distinction has just been drawn between relevant ideas,

---

[1] This note has appeared in *Mind*, N.S. 83, and has been replied to by Dr Schiller in N.S. 84. For my reply see N.S. 85.

[2] N.S. xi.　　　　　　　　　　　[3] *loc. cit.* p. 204.

which are of immediate use, and *irrelevant but true* ideas that are kept in "cold storage" until such time as they become "practically relevant to one of our emergencies." Only when they do this does James seem here to equate the useful and the true, but he is dangerously near the borderline, and in *The Meaning of Truth* we find him explicitly stating the "grotesque conversion" namely, "what works is true and represents a reality for the individual for whom it works[1]."

The conversion is implied even in the paper on *Error* in which it was condemned, for Dr Schiller says, "Truth-claims which have worked badly are condemned as 'errors' *even as those which have worked well are accepted as 'truths*[2].'" Nor is it surprising—apart from his denial— that Dr Schiller should make the assumption, for the whole significance of Pragmatism as a theory of truth, and its claim to both novelty and importance, rests upon the possibility of this conversion. That "all truths work," i.e. are satisfactory from some point of view, no one would contest. The difficulty is to distinguish these "truths" from those other "truth-claims" which satisfy some purpose but are found not to be "true." If, from the fact that "all truths work," it does not follow that "all that works is true," then "working" can *not* be regarded as a test of truth. But it is the peculiar claim of Pragmatism that it does provide such a test; it fails, therefore, just where its claims are greatest.

It is not without justification, therefore, that I have assumed this conversion as a *sine qua non* of the pragmatic theory of truth, since without it the pragmatic theory is both useless and irrelevant, or at best a truism. With it,

---

[1] *op. cit.* p. 243.   [2] *loc. cit.* p. 152. Italics are mine.

unfortunately, according to Dr Schiller's own showing, it is "grotesque."

8. Two questions then arise: What is the Nature of Truth, and what is its criterion? These two questions are hopelessly confused by most "anti-intellectualists," alike by the pragmatist who makes the criterion of truth its nature, and by the Bergsonian Intuitionist who makes its nature its criterion. On the other hand, the distinction is generally recognised by the intellectualist, e.g. by Mr Russell, who discusses the nature of truth but explicitly leaves aside the question of a criterion[1], and by Mr Joachim who definitely states that " A *criterion* of truth—e.g. something other than the truth itself, by which we are to recognise the truth—is not what we require" for "we want to know what truth in its nature is[2]."

The failure to make this vital distinction is, I think, at the root of the collapse of Pragmatism as a theory of truth. The pragmatist argues that there is no quality common to all truths but that of successful working and that in this common quality the nature of truth consists, therefore truth *is* successful working or utility.

But in this confusion of "criterion" with "nature" there is, so it seems to me, a blunder comparable to that which the moralist would make were he to formulate a set of rules for determining whether a given action be right or not, and then were to identify the rules with the Moral Ideal; in other words, just as we can distinguish between casuistry and the Moral Ideal, so we can distinguish between a criterion of truth and the nature of truth; further, just as we can investigate and determine the

---

[1] Philosophical Essays, *The Nature of Truth.*
[2] *Nature of Truth*, p. 67 n.

Moral Ideal while admitting that we are powerless to provide a rule that shall ensure that it *is* carried out in any given case, owing to the complexity of the circumstances that may arise; so we can formulate a theory as to the nature of truth while admitting that it does not of itself supply us with a criterion by which we may know what in any given case is true.

That there is such a blunder is suggested by James' statement that "'The true,' to put it very briefly, is only the expedient in the way of our thinking, just as 'the right' is only the expedient in the way of our behaving[1]."

Now it seems to me that while the two questions cannot be completely severed, nevertheless they not only can but must be treated separately and that the question as to the nature of truth is logically prior to that of its criterion. The pragmatist, of course, who is anxious to reach practical results at once, is more interested in the latter, but he has failed to provide the criterion and we may attribute his failure to the fact that he has not considered the meaning of truth, hence is quite unable to find that quality other than truth by which truth may be known.

It is perhaps unreasonable to imagine that any philosophy can offer such a test or to demand that a winnowing fan be found that will unerringly sever chaff from grain, the true from the false—though, to judge by some of Dr Schiller's utterances, it would seem that Pragmatism makes such a claim. But I ask only—can Pragmatism be held to have attained its goal and fulfilled its promises if it takes up the standpoint adopted by Dr Schiller in his paper on *Error*. That a criterion of truth is discoverable

[1] *Pragmatism*, p. 222.

seems to me extremely doubtful. It is no less than a demand to abolish every form of error save that which shares the nature of lies[1]. Moreover, as we have said, it is necessary first to determine the nature of truth, which Pragmatism has not done, for it does not even distinguish between the two questions.

We have already seen that the Bergsonian intuitionist identifies truth with its criterion, finding them both in " Life," and I have suggested[2] that this view of the nature of truth, which makes it existing reality itself and transfers it from the realm of *knowledge* to that of *being*, dispenses with the need for a criterion the notion of which is valid only within the realm of knowledge.

The identification that the " New Philosophy " makes of " knowing the truth " and " living the real " results, I think, from the fact that M. Bergson makes Duration the stuff, or substance, of Reality itself, and Truth he regards as but another name for Reality. In order then, to know truth the knower must be one with it, inserted within the reality that is to be known. Hence is necessitated the plunge into the " stream of time " or " flux," that constitutes the Bergsonian regression. The knower thereby becomes *part of the flux*—if the spatial metaphor may be allowed—and the distinction between knower and known, knowledge and reality, is abolished. There is no longer Truth but only Reality, which—to use Mr Bradley's phrase—" swallows up " knowledge. But Truth that is lost in the moment of consummation cannot surely be the end in view.

[1] And it is in desperate recognition of this that e.g. Prezzolini says, " The scientist is a liar useful to society ; the liar is a scientist useful to himself " (*Arte di persuadere*, p. 13). James and Schiller, however, have seen fit to separate themselves from such extravagances !

[2] See p. 68 supra.

This is precisely the position in which Bradley lands himself. It is true that he distinguishes between Reality and Truth as an aspect of Reality which "does not as such exist," and for this reason he holds that "truth shows a dissection and never an actual life. Its predicate can never be equivalent to its subject. And, if it became so, and if its adjectives could be at once self-consistent and re-welded to existence it would not be truth any longer[1]." But he seems to regard this non-existent character of Truth, whereby it fails to be "quite identical with reality," as a defect, and he sets up as the goal an Absolute in which all differences are "transformed" and Truth is lost in the flux of sentient experience. His reason for this strange proceeding seems to be precisely similar to Bergson's—the view, namely, that concepts can only analyse and break up the living reality, and thus give only "points of view" and not the concreteness of Reality. They differ in that Bradley holds fast to intellect, while making Reality supra-rational in the form of an Absolute in which Truth is transformed into a higher Reality; whereas Bergson scorns intellect and makes Reality extra-rational in the form of a "vital impulse" prior to the genesis of intellect. In each case knower and known are to be identified, and the problems of knowledge are to be solved by the abolition of knowledge!

The objection that Bradley and Bergson alike feel against a Truth that is "knowledge *about* an other" is due, it seems to me, from their making Truth an Existent. When this is done, then the knower, who is existent, in order to know another existent, viz. Truth, must somehow "enter into it"—as Bergson puts it—and an example can

[1] *Appearance and Reality*, p. 167.

be given—that to know another person completely one must *be* that person—hence, to know anything one must *be* what one knows.

We have already seen[1] that it is on the antithesis between knower and known that knowledge depends, and no satisfactory theory of knowledge could require the abolition of this distinction.

If, however, we admit that Truth is not itself existent, but is a way in which existing things are known, then surely Truth will always be *about an other*, for this is its very nature, and it may be *complete* just because the knower in knowing ceases to be the part that he is as an *existing* knower.

It seems to me, then, that M. Bergson's theory of an intuition in which " the act of knowledge coincides with the generating act of reality[2]," closely resembles Mr Bradley's monistic theory of truth and fails just in the same way, namely, that it seeks an accomplishment that would frustrate its own end, viz. Truth. If, however, it be admitted that knowledge is necessarily, and rightly, dependent upon the distinction of knower and known, it would follow that Truth is always "about an other," and may be complete because it is not an existent.

The basis of this error in M. Bergson's case comes out very clearly in M. Le Roy's treatment of " Truth " as " Life." But Truth is not " life "; it is a way of apprehending life. Nor is philosophy " life," but the interpretation of life by means of reason.

9. Voluntarism springs from distrust of intellect and fear lest " the vital pulse of the human heart " should be

---

[1] p. 148 supra.   [2] *B.S.F.Ph.* 1908, p. 333.

neglected by the philosophers who consider only "some isolated nerve of the intellect[1]."

Further, intellect has failed to solve the problems that metaphysics offers. Voluntarism is a resort to other means than intellect for their solution. Three alternative methods are offered us, which must be very briefly mentioned.

(1) Solution by means of extra-rational choice. This is the method of "Pascal's Wager," the "will to believe" of James, and the "moral method" of Renouvier. It must be remembered that Renouvier himself lays stress on *rational* considerations and only where these fail does he resort to choice. But the method is completed in the "will to believe" and the "Faith Ladder[2]." This pragmatic method, as I pointed out, is identical in principle with Pascal's wager.

(2) Solution by means of action. This is the position of Guyau and Séailles, and constitutes a part of the pragmatic method.

(3) Solution by Intuition. M. Bergson claims that "the return to the immediate takes away contradictions and oppositions in suppressing the problem around which the battle rages," and he adds, "this power of the immediate, I mean its capacity of resolving opposition by suppressing the problem is, in my opinion, the external mark by which the true intuition of the immediate may be recognised[3]."

Of the latter solution we may say at once that the suppression of problems is not equivalent to their solution, and, as M. Bergson's treatment of the problem of free will

[1] Jacks, quoted above, p. 2.
[2] James, *Problems of Philosophy*, Appendix.
[3] *B.S.F.Ph.* 1908, p. 332.

by this method has shown, it is apt to leave the question just where it was before.

Further, the criticism to be passed on each of these three solutions is that they are not "solutions" at all. The antinomies they are supposed to solve are antinomies of reason, hence must be solved by reason. An extra-rational solution cannot be made to meet the case but is merely a confession that the problem is insoluble. Thus the problem of truth remains an intellectual problem and the attempt to solve it "livingly" results in abandoning the quest of truth as such and in substituting for it a conception of life which ignores the interest that gave rise to it. It is then the work of intellect to solve the problems that intellect raises.

We are brought, then, to our final conclusion that philosophy is essentially the affair of intellect, and that "if there is to be a philosophy its proper business is to satisfy the intellect[1]."

This is the position that I would finally endeavour to defend against all forms of Voluntarism, whether they take the position of Pragmatism that the ultimate determinant of truth and solver of problems is will and its desire to believe; or the position of the Intuitionist that unmediated feeling, or extra-rational intuition, is the faculty whereby the real is attained; or the position (close to Pragmatism) that the knot of difficulty is to be cut by action. "Action and the power of life" can *not* solve "those problems to which abstract thought gives rise[2].

But, as Bradley has pointed out, "a merely intellectual harmony is an abstraction" and though it may be admitted

[1] Bradley, *Mind*, N.S. 72, p. 490.   [2] See p. 128 supra.

to be a legitimate abstraction, nevertheless, "if the harmony *were* merely intellectual it would be nothing at all[1]." The satisfaction of intellect is the aim of a true philosophy, but the attainment of its goal will involve more than the satisfaction of *mere* intellect. Such at least is the intellectualist's hope, and if he does not pass at once to the conclusion that all that seems desirable must be real, it is because he sees too much that is not-desirable that has nevertheless none of the marks of illusion. But this is not to abandon the belief—admittedly only a belief—that the harmony is possible of achievement.

Hence, the way to further advance does not lie, it seems to me, in a repudiation of intellect and a resort to extra-intellectual methods, but in a more complete working out of the demands of intellect, i.e. in the development of intellect itself to the full possession of its powers. It is not less trust in intellect that is required to solve its problems, but more, and it is because I believe that intellect in working out its own perfection will not fall short of a harmony that shall fully satisfy all our powers of knowing, striving and loving, that I protest against the pragmatist's condemnation of intellect as involving neglect of "interest" and purpose, and against the Intuitional Mysticism that would make the promised vision obscure and fleeting, hence unable to satisfy the demands of our rational nature.

---

[1] *Appearance and Reality*, 2nd Ed. p. 610.

BIBLIOGRAPHY

A

FRENCH VOLUNTARISTS AND THEIR CHIEF WORKS ARRANGED IN CHRONOLOGICAL ORDER

MAINE DE BIRAN (1766—1824).

L'Influence de l'habitude	1802
Nouvelles Considérations sur les rapports du physique et du moral de l'homme. Ed. Cousin	1834
Oeuvres philosophiques (3 t.). Ed. Cousin	1841
Oeuvres inédites (3 t.). Ed. Naville	1859
Science et Psychologie. Ed. Bertrand	1887

FÉLIX RAVAISSON (1813—1900).

De l'habitude	1832
Essai sur la métaphysique d'Aristote	1837
La Philosophie en France au XIXe siècle	1867
Métaphysique et Morale. Published *R.M.M.* ...	1901

CHARLES RENOUVIER (1818—1903).

Essais de Critique générale (4 Parts)... ...	1854—69
Essais de Critique générale. 2nd Edition enlarged	1875—86
Première Essai : Traité de logique générale (3 t.)	
Deuxième Essai: Traité de Psychologie rationnelle (3 t.)	
Troisième Essai : Les Principes de la Nature (2 t.)	
Classification systématique des doctrines philosophiques (2 t.)	1885—86
Philosophie analytique de l'histoire (4 t.) ...	1896—97
La Nouvelle Monadologie	1899
Les Dilemmes de la Métaphysique pure	1901
Le Personnalisme	1903

ALFRED FOUILLÉE (1838—1912).

La Liberté et le Déterminisme (1st Ed.)	1872
L'Idée moderne du Droit	1878
L'Avenir de la Métaphysique	1887
Evolutionnisme des Idées-forces	1890
Psychologie des Idées-forces	1893
La Pensée et les nouvelles écoles anti-intellectualistes	1911

JEAN MARIE GUYAU (1854—1888).

Esquisse d'une Morale sans obligation ni sanction ...	1885
L'Irreligion de l'Avenir	1887
La Genèse de l'idée de temps (published posthumously)	1890

HENRI POINCARÉ (1854—1912).

La Science et l'Hypothèse	1903
La Valeur de la Science	1904
Science et Méthode	1908

EMILE BOUTROUX (1845—   ).

De la Contingence des Lois de la Nature	1875
De l'Idée de Loi Naturelle dans la Science et dans la Philosophie contemporaine	1895
La Science et la Religion dans la Philosophie contemporaine	1908

HENRI BERGSON (1852—   ).

(i) *Books.*

Essai sur les Données Immédiates de la Conscience E. Tr. under title *Time and Free Will*, by F. L. Pogson, 1910.	1889
Matière et Mémoire : essai sur la relation du corps avec l'esprit ... . E. Tr. by N. M. Paul and W. Scott Palmer, 1911.	1896
Le Rire : essai sur la signification du comique ...	1900
Introduction à la Métaphysique. *R.M.M.* ... ... E. Tr. by T. E. Hulme, 1912.	1903
L'Evolution Créatrice ... ... E. Tr. by Arthur Mitchell, 1911.	1907

HENRI BERGSON (*contd.*).

La Perception du Changement : conférences faites à
l'université d'Oxford   1911

(ii) *Articles.*

Le parallelisme psycho-physique et la métaphysique
positive. *B.S.F.* (June)   1901
L'Effort intellectuel. *Revue philosophique* (Jan.) ...   1902
Le paralogisme psycho-physiologique. *R.M.M.* (Nov.)   1904
Esprit et Matière. *B.S.F.* (p. 94—99)   1905
Notice sur la vie et les oeuvres de M. Félix Ravaisson-
Mollien. *Mémoires de l'Académie des Sciences
morales et politiques*   1907
A propos de l'évolution de l'intelligence géométrique.
R.M.M. , ...   1908
Sur l'influence de sa philosophie sur les élèves des
lycées. *B.S.F.* (p. 21—22)   1908
Note sur le mot *immédiat. B.S.F.* (Aug.)   1908
Le Souvenir du présent et la fausse reconnaissance.
Rv. phil. (Dec.)   1908
Life and Consciousness. *Hibbert Journal* (Oct.) ...   1911
L'Intuition philosophique. *R.M.M.* (Nov.)   1911

(iii) *References.*

A. D. Lindsay. The Philosophy of Bergson   ...   1911
J. M'Kellar Stewart. A Critical Exposition of
Bergson's Philosophy   1911
J. Solomon. Bergson. (Philosophies Ancient and
Modern Series.)   1911
D. Balsillie. An Examination of Professor Bergson's
Philosophy   1912
H. Wildon Carr. Henri Bergson : The Philosophy of
Change. (People's Books.)   1912
E. Le Roy. Une Philosophie nouvelle : Henri Bergson   1912
Hugh S. R. Elliot. Modern Science and the Illusions
of Professor Bergson, with preface by Sir Ray
Lankester   1912

MAURICE BLONDEL (b. circ. 1870).
L'Action   1894

LACHELIER.
Du fondement de l'Induction   1896

LABERTHONNIÈRE (b. circ. 1872).
Essais de philosophie religieuse   1901

EDOUARD LE ROY (b. circ. 1872).
Science et Philosophie. *R.M.M.*   ...   ...   1899—1900
Un positivisme nouveau. *R.M.M.*   1901
Sur la logique de l'invention. *R.M.M.*   1907
Dogme et Critique   1907

JOSEPH WILBOIS (b. circ. 1880).
La Méthode des Sciences physiques. *R.M.M.*   1890—1900
L'Esprit positif. *R.M.M.*   ...   .   1901—1902

B

ANGLO-AMERICAN PRAGMATISTS AND THEIR
CHIEF WORKS

C. S. PEIRCE.
How to make our Ideas Clear. *Popular Science
    Monthly*, vol. XII.   ...   .   1877—78
Pragmatism and Pragmaticism. *Monist*, vol. XV. (Oct.)   1905

WILLIAM JAMES (ob. 1910).
The Will to Believe. Essays   1897
Philosophical Conceptions and Practical Results :
    address delivered at Berkeley, Aug. 26th   ...   1898
Varieties of Religious Experience   1902
Pragmatism   1907
The Meaning of Truth. (Articles reprinted)   ...   1909
A Pluralistic Universe   1909
Some Problems of Philosophy (published posthumously)   1911

F. C. S. SCHILLER.

    Axioms as Postulates *in Personal Idealism.* Ed.
        H. Sturt   1902

    Humanism   1903

    Studies in Humanism   1907

    Plato or Protagoras ? Being a critical examination of
        the Protagoras Speech in the *Theaetetus* with some
        remarks upon Error...   1908

    Error. *Proceedings of the Aristotelian Society,* N.S. xi   1910

G. PREZZOLINI.

    L'Arte di Persuadere   1907

C

GENERAL REFERENCES

DESCARTES.

    Oeuvres Complètes. Ed. Adam et Tannery   1898—1910

    The Philosophical Works of Descartes. Haldane and
        Ross (2 vols.)...   ...   .   1911—1912

MALEBRANCHE.

    De la Recherche de la Vérité   1712

PASCAL.

    Pensées. Ed. Brunschvicg   1896

CONDILLAC.

    Traité des Sensations   1798

DESTUTT DE TRACY.

    Éléments d'Idéologie   1801

A. COMTE.

    Cours de Philosophie Positive   1894

    Discours sur l'esprit Positif   1898

ALEXIS BERTRAND.

    La Psychologie de l'Effort   1889

L. P. JACKS.

    The Alchemy of Thought   1910

F. H. BRADLEY.

    Appearance and Reality. 2nd Ed.   1908

INDEX OF NAMES

For EU product safety concerns, contact us at Calle de José Abascal, 56–1°,
28003 Madrid, Spain or eugpsr@cambridge.org.

www.ingramcontent.com/pod-product-compliance
Ingram Content Group UK Ltd.
Pitfield, Milton Keynes, MK11 3LW, UK
UKHW020315140625
459647UK00018B/1886